Integrating Technology and Pedagogy in Physical Education Teacher Education

Melanie Mitchell
Robert McKethan

Bonnie's Fitware Inc.
Cerritos, California

Library of Congress Control Number

Mitchell, Melanie
McKethan, Robert
Integrating technology and pedagogy in physical education teacher education, 1st /
Melanie Mitchell and Robert McKethan

ISBN 1-893166-99-6
1. Physical education and training–Computer-assisted instruction.
2. Educational technology. 3. Media programs (Education)

Library of Congress Control Number: 2002117790

Copyright ©2003 by Bonnie's Fitware Inc.

Copyeditor: Carol A. Bruce

Printed in the United States of America

Bonnie's Fitware Inc.
18832 Stefani Ave
Cerritos, CA 90703
419-828-2144
www.pesoftware.com

Table of Contents

Reviewers

Susan M. Barnd Ed.D.

Assistant Professor

Exercise and Sport Science

University of Wisconsin - La Crosse

Robert J. Smith, Ph.D.

Associate Professor

Department of Movement Studies and Exercise Science

East Stroudsburg University

Deborah A. Wuest, Ed.D.

Professor

Department of Health Promotion and Human Movement

Ithaca College

Preface

This book provides guidance for modeling the use of technology in physical education teacher education programs (PETE). The NASPE/NCATE Beginning Teacher Standards (NASPE/NCATE BTS) list and describe the competencies that are expected of preservice teachers. Similarly, the National Education Technology Standards for Teachers (NETS-T) provide guidelines for what the induction phase teacher should know and be able to do when using technology as a resource for planning, instruction, and assessment. To facilitate the process, this book illustrates the relationships between the NASPE/NCATE BTS and the NETS-T.

Physical education is a part of the total curriculum. Although physical education focuses primarily on teaching and learning in the psychomotor domain, it also contributes to the cognitive and affective domains of learning. Physical education has the potential–as does any curriculum–to contribute to student understanding of the culture, to transmit social values, and to meet the needs of individuals in order to create a better world.

Games, competitive activities, dance, and physical activity allow students to experience cultures, rituals, and festivities that are related to the different ethnic groups represented in American society. These kinds of activities provide teachers with opportunities to include lessons about the people, places, and times where the activities originate. Affective outcomes include learning to work efficiently as part of a group, learning how to respond to conflict, and learning how to solve problems.

Physical education is a significant partner in the total school curriculum. Although physical education is viewed by many in the lay community and the education profession as a non-academic subject, it does in fact have the potential to promote academic as well as skill learning through a predominately psychomotor domain. Cognitive learning is addressed in the areas of exercise physiology, biomechanics, motor development, historical perspectives, aesthetics, and–most significantly–motor learning (the ability to "learn how to learn"). Adoption of technology as a learning tool by physical educators advances the perception of physical education as an equal partner in the total curriculum, a partner that prepares children to live in a rapidly changing global community.

The reader will notice that two basic resources provide the conceptual underpinnings for this document: the NETS-T, and the NASPE/NCATE BTS. Although it may appear at first glance that there is no relationship between the two documents, both address the initial competencies expected of beginning teachers. This is important, because many preservice teachers fail to see or understand how technology can support teaching in physical education. There also is a direct link in that the NASPE/NCATE BTS includes, as one of its 10 standards, a yardstick that addresses technology competencies for physical educators.

The NETS-T details performance competencies for preservice and inservice teachers. The NETS-T was created to support teacher education programs in developing preservice teachers' technology skills which enables their use of technology skills in the instructional processes.

The National Educational Technology Standards for Students (NETS-S) provide a description of technology competencies for PK-12 students. Competencies for PK-12 students focus on the operation of technology, using appropriate technology terms in communication, cooperative and ethical behaviors when using technology, taking care of technology, using devices such as digital cameras, and gathering information through the use of telecommunications. Although the focus of this book is not to address NETS-S, it is important for physical education teacher educators to utilize these standards as a part of preservice teachers' educational experiences. Integration of the NETS-S into preservice teacher experience promotes the likelihood that later, as practicing professionals, they will deliver appropriate technology-based experiences to their students.

The NASPE document, *Moving into the Future: National Standards for Physical Education,* is a comprehensive guide to outcomes-based instruction in physical education (1995). It identifies content standards based on the characteristics of a physically educated person, which were developed in 1992. It also provides a grade-level curricular emphasis for each of the seven content standards. Sample benchmarks are identified, along with assessment examples.

Although there is no direct reference to the use of technology in the NASPE content standards, the use of technology is implicitly embedded in the assessment examples. In addition, the use of technology facilitates instructional presentation and the development and implementation of assessments as well as the storage and recall of student performance data.

Chapter 1 defines the term "technology". It describes the growth of information and our need to use tools effectively and efficiently. It also shows the growth of technology in the 20th century. Technology tools are categorized according to how they are used in the educational process.

Chapters 2 and 3 provide an overview of the development of the NASPE/NCATE BTS and the NETS-T, respectively. Chapter 3 also provides a brief description of the NETS-S.

Chapter 4 shows how the NASPE/NCATE BTS align with the NETS-T. The NASPE/NCATE BTS and the NETS-T are aligned according to each NASPE/NCATE competency. The reader will notice that sometimes multiple NETS-T standards are aligned to the NASPE/NCATE BTS. Instructional activities are identified as a part of the alignment document.

Chapter 5 develops lesson plans from selected instructional activities found in Chapter 4. These lesson plans illustrate the integration of technology and teaching processes in physical education for teacher educators, preservice teachers, and inservice teachers. Chapter 5 presents sample lesson plans for each of the NASPE/NCATE BTS and links them to the suggested activities found in Chapter 4.

In brief, this book focuses on the growing need to use technology in physical education. It defines technology and provides examples of educational technology. It integrates competencies–both instructional and technological–in an easy-to-understand format. Although the book provides integrated lesson examples, its primary purpose is to provide ideas that will assist the teacher educator in developing instructional experiences that support both the NASPE/NCATE BTS and the NETS-T.

References

International Society for Technology in Education. (2002). *National educational technology standards for teachers.* Eugene, OR: International Society for Technology in Education.

National Association for Sport and Physical Education. (1995). *Moving into the future: National Standards for physical education.* Boston, MA: WCB McGraw-Hill.

Chapter 1
The Digital Age

With each new day we become more aware of the digital/information age in which we live. Information is increasing in exponential proportions. Descriptions of this ever growing phenomenon help us to understand the enormity of information in the digital age. For example, Anglin (1995) cites the volume of information generated on an annual basis in the biomedical field. He asserts that it would take 22 centuries to read the biomedical literature generated in one year. Anglin's point was validated in a 1996 speech about the information age by Davidson, who stated that, "... more information is generated in a 24-hour period than you could take in for the rest of your life. And, as more people go online and add information to the Internet, we will rapidly approach a situation in which more information is generated on earth in one hour than you could take in for the rest of your life."

As the volume of information has increased, the cost of technology for managing that information has dropped dramatically. Consider that, in 1970, the cost of transmitting the Encyclopaedia Britannica across America as an electronic data file would have been $187. In the 21st century, the cost of transmitting the entire contents of the Library of Congress across America would be $40 (Szabo, 2001). The good news for consumers and educators is that, as the cost of technology spirals down, technology becomes easier to obtain.

Because information is growing in exponential proportions, there is an increasing need to filter, identify, judge, and utilize information that supports learning. Teachers and students alike now have equal access to information that previously was unavailable. It is imperative that we take advantage of the available tools to help us become efficient and effective learners.

Educators also must become proficient in using any device or process that supports efficiency. We must be able to identify potential sources of information relevant to teaching; we must acquire the skills to efficiently sort and evaluate the usefulness of the information; and we must utilize the tools that support the application of the information in our teacher education programs.

Predictions suggest that society will become more dependent upon technology as we move further into the 21st century. One consequence of this dependency is a shift toward what Pearson (2000) termed, a "care economy." This simply means that we begin to focus more on the person side of activity. In a sense, the mission of physical education has always been about the person. Pearson's prediction about the people side of activity as a result of our increasing dependency on technology has implications for teaching in physical education. Physical educators must use the tools that are available to support learning, physical activity and–ultimately–the individual.

Silverman (1997) suggests that one problem our profession faces is the failure of teacher educators to model the use of technology in their classes. If we assume that preservice teachers value the methods, content, and behavior modeled in teacher education programs, then teacher educators must model the use of technology with the expectation that preservice teachers will use technology in their own instructional practice. Herein lies the challenge: Teacher educators must practice what they preach!

Technology Defined

People who were born after 1975 tend to think about technology in terms of computers, software, the Internet, and ancillary tools that have as their basis some form of computer technology. For those from earlier generations, concepts of technology might include telephone, radio, and television. As we think of the tools used by the present generation we begin to realize that technology is not limited to computers and their plethora of microchip driven tools. Rather, it is a term for processes in which human beings engage themselves in order to increase their control of the material environment and to solve problems (Anglin, 1995; TechWeb, 2002).

Computer technology (and microchips) can be found in a variety of contemporary tools such as (but not limited to) children's books, toys, automobiles, medical equipment, lighting, and telephones. Even with the prevalence of computer-based tools, however, it is important for the reader to understand that technology is not limited to the use of computers to control one's world or to solve one's problems. Technology includes any device that makes our jobs and lives easier.

The 20th century has witnessed epic events, including the flight of the Wright Brothers in 1903, and the landing of men on the moon in 1969. Many significant technologies have emerged. These noteworthy developments are described in the following paragraphs.

Technology in the early 20th century focused on visual mechanisms such as the motion picture projector, which was preceded in 1894 by the Vitascope. The Vitascope was significant because it allowed for the projection of colored motion pictures (Saettler, 1990). A number of companies developed motion picture projectors in the early 20th century.

The first commercial radio station, KDKA in Pittsburgh, went on the air in 1920. Radio provided listeners with entertainment as well as information about significant happenings in the world. Radio enabled listeners to have more immediate access to breaking news such as the crash of the Hindenburg, the Japanese attack on Pearl Harbor, and the landing of Allied troops at Normandy during World War II (Stark, 1994).

During World War II, the military used slide projectors, overhead projectors, and audio devices in training programs such as aircraft and ship recognition as well as foreign language instruction (Saettler, 1990).

Television resulted from the work of inventors in a number of different countries. The British Broadcasting Corporation (BBC) aired programs at night starting in 1929. Prior to World War II, in 1935, the Germans claimed to be the first country to make television broadcasts available to the public (Whitaker, 1989).

Prior to World War II, the Federal Communications Commission began licensing television stations on a commercial basis. After a suspension of licensing during the war, commercial licensing resumed with great excitement. The first venture into educational television took place in 1945. Television stations began broadcasting on channels specifically allocated for educational television in 1953 (Saettler, 1990).

The computer also had its genesis during World War II. Germany and the United States developed computers to assist in the design of airplanes and missiles, and to calculate artillery trajectories. The ENAIC computer, developed in 1946, was 1,000 times faster than other computers developed at about the same time. Since that time, there have been many computer milestones, such as personal computers, Windows-type operating systems, personal digital assistants, and the Internet.

In addition to these more visible technologies, there are many other significant technologies that are "married" to computing. These include cable, fiber optics, videodiscs, and satellites that are designed to help people have greater control over their environment (Nugent, 1987). Historically, technologies developed for non-educational world are adopted for use in the education world.

Educational Technology

Educational technology reflects the generic definition of technology as tools or means of solving problems. And, much like the more generic term, it has many definitions that go beyond computers. Educational technology is defined as, "...processes that involve people, procedures, ideas, devices, and organizations for analyzing problems, and devising, implementing, evaluating, and managing solutions to those problems..." (ABCT Task Force, 1977). This generation-old definition of technology continues to be supported by current educational professionals.

The diversity embedded in the term "technology" also is found in contemporary educational technology. Serdiukov (2000) uses a number of terms to define subsets of educational technology. They include:

-Technical tools – computer hardware.

-Programming tools – software.

-Didactic tools – textbooks, courseware.

-Method tools – instructional methods and techniques.

The International Society for Technology in Education (ISTE, 2002) delivers a definition of technology that is similar, although more narrowly focused than the preceding definitions. ISTE defines technology-based instruction as instructional applications that involve some aspect of computers or related technologies. A broader definition of technology imbedded within this is that technology is a tool, much like other tools that support managing the world and its information resources.

It is our assumption that the advent of educational technology took place where and when learning activities took place. Certainly, this point becomes evident as we see the movement of learning from the home, to the one-room schoolhouse, to community-based schools, to consolidated schools. Technological tools that were developed for reasons other than education–tools such as television, cameras, and computers–began to support the educational process.

The following examples show that technology is a process as well as a device. In each case, the example includes methods or processes designed to make the educational process more efficient and effective:

1. Desks with writing surfaces.
2. Writing slates for copying.
3. Sequencing of instruction.*
4. Criterion-referenced testing.*
5. Film.
6. Television.
7. Audio and video recordings.
8. Computers for instruction and information management.

Instructional methods or testing methods are not devices, yet they are representative of technology because they facilitate instruction and learning.

Physical Education and Technology

Mohnsen (2001), in the preface to *Using Technology in Physical Education,* 3rd *Edition*, tracks the definitions of educational technology illustrated in the previous section. She defines technology as tools that help teachers become more efficient with their time, and as an alternative way to provide instruction for students. For the purpose of this book, technology is the tools or devices used to create educational materials, to facilitate learning, to generate products of learning, and to introduce greater efficiency in managing the educational environment.

Table 1 lists current technology that can be used by physical educators. The column headings are based on Serdiukov's (2000) classifications of educational technology. The technical category refers to hardware. Our interpretation of hardware is broad based and includes not only computer hardware but also handheld computers, fax machines, televisions, and monitors.

The technical classification of tools supports the educational process in the following ways:
1. Computers run browser and email software to communicate and retrieve information via email attachment or retrieval from the Internet.
2. Computers run software such as word processors, spreadsheets, and certificate makers to develop instructional materials.
3. Computers address another hardware function as they store student data and instructional materials.
4. Televisions are an example of hardware that can receive signals that display educational programs.
5. Videocassette recorders and DVD players are examples of hardware that can be used to deliver material that supports the learning process.

Programming devices include software that is used to create lesson plans, instructional materials such as task cards, scoring rubrics, certificates, assessment instruments, and displays that support the instructional process. Software tools support not only the development of instructional materials, but also products of student learning.

Teachers and students use didactic tools to construct learning experiences. Serdiukov's (2000) definition of didactic tools pertains to courseware. For the purposes of this book, didactic tools also include a wide range of objects including, but not limited to, stethoscopes, assistive technology, educational TV, and simulation games.

The last category–methodological technology–is probably not generally considered to be a technology. This category addresses instructional methods designed to support student learning or to support specific learning competencies. For example, if the teacher's identified learning competencies are associated with higher order thinking skills, then the activities may focus not on recall but on activities requiring analysis, evaluation, or synthesis of ideas.

Another example of methodological technology is the use of teaching by invitation. Teaching by invitation is a teaching method that acknowledges that students can make decisions about their own learning. For example, when using throwing and catching skills in an application activity, students are given the invitation to choose the object with which they feel they can be most successful. Students are allowed to choose between a beanbag, a four-inch rubber utility ball, a whiffle ball, or a four-inch gator ball. In each example, the processes used involve technology, because these processes facilitate instruction and learning.

The lists found in Table 1.1 are not exhaustive. However, as we think about devices we call technology and devices that support student learning, we begin to see the vast storehouse of tools that are available to physical education teacher educators.

In a prediction about future learning in physical education, Taylor and Saverance (1990) describe a physical education class. They write of credit card sized storage devices with capacities approaching one gigabyte. They describe a game called Laser Tag and tablets for receiving and displaying information. Exercise and nutritional information used in this future class can be downloaded. It has been 13 years since Taylor and Saverance described the future of physical education. The future is here!

As teacher educators, we are obligated to prepare our students to teach the next generation of students. Our success is dependent upon our understanding of the role of technology in our living. We must be mindful that physical education is a part of "our living."

The success of our efforts also is dependent on how we use the relevant tools to support and facilitate learning. As we consider the use of technology and teaching, we must begin to see the relationship between abilities or competencies in the use of technology devices and the processes, behaviors, and methods that are associated with effective teaching. The chapters which follow describe the framework for successful teaching–the NASPE/NCATE Beginning Teacher Standards (BTS) and the NETS-T– and illustrate the relationships that exist between the use of technology and teaching processes.

Table 1.1
Physical Education Technology Tools

Technical

Computers
Scanners
Digital Cameras
Digital Camcorders
Printers
Conventional Cameras
Fax Machines
Video Capture Boards
Handheld Computers
Laminating Machines
CD ROM Burners
External Storage Devices
Photo Copiers
VCR Players
Electronic Scoreboards
CD Players
DVD Players
Slide Projectors
Audio Tape Players
Two-way Players
Opaque Projectors
Data Projectors
Televisions/Monitors
Telephones
White Boards

Didactic Tools

Internet Browsers
Textbooks
Courseware (Textbook Support)
Video
Tutorial Software
Drill and Practice Software
Transparencies
Stopwatches
Microscopes
Game Simulation
Virtual Reality
GPS Devices
Metronomes
Educational TV
Heart Rate Monitors
Calorie Counters
PowerPoint Presentations
Compasses
Blood Pressure Cuffs
Anatomical Software
Online Courses
Online Journals
Assistive Technology (Voice Amplification)
Stethoscopes
Skinfold Calipers
Sit-and-Reach Boxes

Programming Tools

Microsoft Word
Microsoft Excel
Microsoft Access
Microsoft PowerPoint
Snag-it (Screen Capture) Software
Calendar Software
Puzzle Maker Software
Clip Art Software
Nutritional Analysis Software
Body Composition Software
Behavior Management Software
WebCt
Blackboard
IEP Software
Certificate Makers
Teacher Observation Software
Data Analysis Software
Web Page Design Software
Photo Editing Software

Methodological Tools

Methods of Questioning
Teaching Styles
Curriculum Models
Integrated Teaching
Teaching by Invitation
Intra-task Variation
Checking for Understanding
Feedback
Sustaining Feedback
Methods of Organizing Class
Alignment of Content, Objectives,
    and Assessments

References

ABCT Task Force. (1977). *Educational technology: Definition and glossary of terms*. Washington, DC: Association for Educational Communications and Technology.

Anglin, E. (1995). *Instructional technology: Past, present, and future* (2nd ed.). Englewood, CO: Libraries Unlimited.

Computer History Museum. *Timeline of computer history.* Accessed December 17, 2002, at: http://www.computerhistory.org.

Davidson, J. (1996). The shortcomings of the information age: Handling information overload. *Vital Speeches*, 62, 495-503.

International Society of Technology in Education. (2002). *National educational technology standards for teachers*. Eugene, OR: Author.

Mohnsen, B. S. (2001). *Using technology in physical education,* (3rd ed.). Cerritos, CA: Bonnie's Fitware.

National Association for Sport and Physical Education. (2001). *Standards for initial programs in physical education teacher education*. Reston, VA: Author. Available at: http://www.aahperd.org/naspe/pdf_files/standards_initial.pdf.

Nugent, G. C. (1987). Innovations in telecommunications. In R. M. Gagne (Ed.), *Instructional technology foundations*. Hillsdale, NJ: Lawrence Erlbaum Associates.

Pearson, I. D. (2000). The next 20 years in technology: Timeline and commentary. *The Futurist*, January-February, 14-19.

Saettler, P. (1990). *The evolution of American educational technology*. Englewood, CO: Libraries Unlimited.

Serdiukov, P. (2000). *Terminology of educational technology: A quantitative study based on SITE conference proceedings*. 2000 (1). 1624-1629., Norfolk, VA: Association for the Advancement of Computing in Education (AACE). Accessed at: http://www.aace.org/dl/index.cfm/fuseaction/advancedsearch.

Stark, P. (1994). *A History of Radio Broadcasting*. Accessed at: http://www.kcmetro.cc.mo.us/pennvalley/biology/lewis/crosby/bilboard.htm.

Silverman, S. (1997). Technology and physical education: Present possibilities and potential problems. *Quest*, 49, 306-314.

Szabo, M. (2001). *The information revolution and the future role of educators*. Society for Information Technology and Teacher Education, 2001, 563-569. Available at: http://www.aaco.org/dl/Search/view.cfm?id=3570.

Taylor, M. S., & Saverance, D. P. (1990). Computers, physical education, and the year 2000. *Journal of Health, Physical Education, Recreation and Dance*, 66, 38-39.

TechWeb. *TechEncyclopedia*. Accessed December 17, 2002, at: http://www.techweb.com/encyclopedia/defineterm?term=technology&x=14&y=11.

Whitaker, J. (1989). *Milestones in the evolution of technology*. Available at: http://inventors.about.com/gi/dynamic/offsite.htm?site=http://www.tvhandbook.com/History/History.htm.

Chapter 2
Overview of NASPE and NCATE Standards

The public expects teachers to have the knowledge of appropriate curriculum content and effective teaching capabilities that will allow them to help all students become competent and informed individuals and productive members of society. In short, teachers must ensure that all students learn. The reform movement of the past 15 years has resulted in the establishment of national education standards for all curricular areas, including physical education. These standards do not dictate a specific national curriculum or a predetermined course of study, but they do include competencies that all young people, grades K-12, should have upon completion of school. In other words, these standards define what our children should know and be able to do as a result of their education.

NASPE Standards

The National Association for Sport and Physical Education (NASPE) established an Outcomes Committee. Its charge was to formulate a definition of a physically educated person (see Table 2.1). According to this definition, a physically educated person has learned how to perform the motor skills necessary to participate in different physical activities, maintains physical fitness by participating in physical activity regularly, knows the importance of being physically active, and values the contributions physical activity makes to a healthful lifestyle (NASPE, 1992). The definition was later expanded to include physical education content standards (see Table 2.2) and sample benchmarks for selected grade levels (NASPE, 1995).

The NASPE content standards define what a student in physical education should know and be able to do as a result of a quality physical education program. These standards identify the knowledge, physical skills, attitudes, and behaviors that are essential to successful student learning in the physical education discipline.

Table 2.1: Definition of a Physically Educated Person

A physically educated person:

1. **HAS** learned skills necessary to perform a variety of physical activities.
2. **IS** physically fit.
3. **DOES** participate regularly in physical activity.
4. **KNOWS** the implications of and the benefits from involvement in physical activities.
5. **VALUES** physical activity and its contribution to a healthful lifestyle in order to pursue a lifetime of healthful physical activity.

Reprinted from *Moving Into the Future: National Standards for Physical Education* (1995) with permission from the National Association for Sport and Physical Education (NASPE), 1900 Association Drive, Reston, VA 20191-1599.

Table 2.2: NASPE Content Standards for Students

A physically educated person:

1. Demonstrates competency in many movement forms and proficiency in a few movement forms.
2. Applies movement concepts and principles to the learning and development of motor skills.
3. Exhibits a physically active lifestyle.
4. Achieves and maintains a health enhancing level of physical fitness.
5. Demonstrates responsible personal and social behavior in physical activity settings.
6. Demonstrates understanding and respect for differences among people in physical activity settings.
7. Understands that physical activity provides opportunities for enjoyment, challenge, self-expression, and social interaction.

Reprinted from *Moving Into the Future: National Standards for Physical Education* (1995) with permission from the National Association for Sport and Physical Education (NASPE), 1900 Association Drive, Reston, VA 20191-1599.

National Council for Accreditation of Teacher Education

As a result of the educational reform movement and the development of national standards for students, the need arose for national standards for teachers, including preservice teachers. The National Council for Accreditation of Teacher Education (NCATE)–a coalition of several specialty professional associations including NASPE, teachers, teacher educators, content specialists, and policy makers–has approved several sets of program standards, including the national physical education standards. The teacher standards adopted by NCATE were designed to ensure that teachers are prepared to help students obtain the competencies, skills, and knowledge necessary to become knowledgeable and productive members of society. The standards reinforce the importance of teachers acquiring knowledge of content or subject matter, effectively teaching others, and helping all students learn. The NASPE/NCATE Beginning Teacher Standards (NASPE/NCATE BTS) are described in the section below.

NASPE Beginning Teacher Standards

NASPE developed the Beginning Teacher Standards, which have been adopted by NCATE, to serve as guidelines in preparing physical educators to teach children in grades K-12 (NASPE, 1995; NASPE, 2001). The NASPE/NCATE BTS define the knowledge and skills associated with teaching and the physical education content that is essential in the development of effective teachers (see Table 2.3).

In 2001, NASPE added a tenth standard–Technology–to the original nine. Technology was included to reflect its increased usage in educational settings. Each of the NASPE standards is described in the sections below.

BTS 1: Content Knowledge

Preservice teachers need to understand not only the physical education content, but the pedagogical content as well. Physical education content involves knowing the critical elements of the skills taught, being able to perform those skills, being able to develop appropriate sequences to enhance skill learning, and being able to apply bioscience theory and concepts to enhance skill learning. Preservice teachers also must understand the current physical education issues, laws, and national standards. These competencies represent the specific content and skill knowledge necessary to provide appropriate instruction in physical education classes.

Table 2.3: NASPE/NCATE Beginning Teacher Standards

Standard 1	Content Knowledge
Standard 2	Growth and Development
Standard 3	Diverse Students
Standard 4	Management and Motivation
Standard 5	Communication
Standard 6	Planning and Instruction
Standard 7	Student Assessment
Standard 8	Reflection
Standard 9	Technology
Standard 10	Collaboration

Reprinted from *National Standards for Beginning Physical Education Teachers* (1995) with permission from the National Association for Sport and Physical Education (NASPE), 1900 Association Drive, Reston, VA 20191-1599.

BTS 2: Growth and Development

This standard focuses on the preservice teacher being able to understand the developmental stages of learning and growing–including the biological, psychological, sociological, experiential, and environmental factors–in order to design safe and appropriate learning experiences for students in grades PK-12. In order to design effective learning environments, preservice teachers will need to observe students performing skills and assess their proficiency levels in the physical, affective, and cognitive domains.

BTS 3: Diverse Students

Preservice teachers also must be able to recognize that students are unique individuals who do not learn material in the same manner. Based on these differences, preservice teachers must know how to provide appropriate instruction using a variety of teaching methods.

BTS 4: Management and Motivation

Preservice teachers must develop good management skills and become effective managers. Management involves establishing and maintaining structure in an environment that is conducive to learning. A good manager incorporates strategies that focus on providing a safe, positive, and structured learning environment in which students want to learn.

Motivation also is a key component that affects learning. If preservice teachers can determine some of the reasons why students learn or why they behave differently or respond differently to different stimuli, then they will be in a better position to influence learning. In order to begin to understand these differences and to influence learning, preservice teachers will need to develop appropriate strategies to motivate students to participate and learn physical education skills.

BTS 5: Communication

Preservice teachers usually acquire the skills they need to provide the initial communication of what to do and how to do it rather quickly, because communication of what to do and how to do it is typically associated with teaching physical education (Rink, 2002). Preservice teachers need to demonstrate their abilities to communicate in many different ways, including verbal and nonverbal ways. In addition to being able to demonstrate communication skills themselves, preservice teachers also need to foster communication skills among their students.

BTS 6: Planning and Instruction

Planning is an integral component of the teaching/learning process. In the planning process, preservice teachers identify curriculum goals and objectives as well as daily lesson objectives. The planning process allows preservice teachers to ensure that they are providing developmentally appropriate lessons.

Preservice teachers also need to understand pedagogical content in order to provide a developmentally appropriate learning environment. The content is based on the national, state, and local physical education standards.

BTS 7: Student Assessment

Assessment is another crucial component of the teaching/learning process. Preservice teachers need to understand and be able to use a variety of assessment practices to determine if students have achieved the goals and objectives set forth in the lesson, to provide feedback about student performance, and to guide instruction. The preservice teacher also must be able to interpret and use the data collected from assessments to make informed instructional decisions.

BTS 8: Reflection

Not only do effective teachers make decisions relating to the teaching process, they also reflect on their decisions and what happens in their classes as a result of those decisions. According to this standard, preservice teachers should engage in the reflective teaching cycle in which they analyze their teaching, identify the strengths and weaknesses, and set goals for improvement.

BTS 9: Technology

The preservice teacher needs to develop the knowledge and skills to implement current technologies that can be incorporated into the physical education learning environment. Preservice teachers also should be able to design technology enhanced learning environments and use technologies to communicate with others.

BTS 10: Collaboration

Effective physical educators also establish positive relationships with others in the field and outside the field. They become advocates for their program and for the importance of physical education to the development of the whole child. This standard focuses on the preservice teacher developing relationships with colleagues, parents, and community agencies to foster student learning.

Summary

The NASPE content standards (NASPE, 1995) and the NASPE/NCATE BTS (NASPE, 2001) are essential components in the establishment of quality physical education programs. The focus of a quality physical education program is on student attainment of the NASPE Content Standards. Through the attainment of these goals, students can become physically educated individuals who live a healthy lifestyle. In addition, effective preservice teachers are those who are able to meet the NASPE/NCATE BTS. Preservice teachers who meet these standards are capable of offering developmentally appropriate activities that ultimately result in a quality physical education program.

References

International Society of Technology in Education. (2002). *National educational technology standards for teachers*. Eugene, OR: Author. Available at: http://www.ncate.org.

National Association for Sport and Physical Education. (1992). *Outcomes of quality physical education programs.* Reston, VA: Author.

National Association for Sport and Physical Education. (1995). *Moving into the future: National Physical Education Standards: A guide to content and assessment.* Reston, VA: Author.

National Association for Sport and Physical Education. (2001). *Standards for initial programs in physical education teacher education.* Reston, VA: Author. Available at: http://www.aahperd.org/naspe/ pdf_files/standards_initial.pdf.

Rink, J. (2002). Teaching *physical education for learning, 4th Edition*. New York, NY: McGraw-Hill.

Chapter 3
Overview of National Education Technology Standards

The use of technology in education has increased dramatically during the past decade. Technologies ranging from cameras to computers have been integrated into the teaching/learning process. The International Society for Technology in Education (ISTE) initiated the National Educational Technology Standards (NETS) project in 2002. The ISTE goal in the development of NETS was to advocate the appropriate use of technology in educational settings and to support and improve learning, teaching, and administration.

The members of this organization are leaders in educational technology, teacher educators, personnel from state departments of public instruction, curriculum and technology specialists, and teachers. ISTE supports all educational curriculum areas by providing technology information, technology resources, and curriculum ideas. The NETS project's mission is to develop national educational technology standards for students, teachers, and administrators to use as guidelines in helping individuals become technology literate.

The conceptual framework for implementing and applying technology in the educational environment has been established through NETS for students (1998), NETS for teachers (2000), and NETS for administrators (2002). The goal of each set of NETS standards and resources is to help teachers, students, and administrators understand what they should know and be able to do with technology in order to become competent, technology literate individuals (ISTE, 2002). The following sections provide an overview of the goals and standards of the NETS for students (NETS-S) and the NETS for teachers (NETS-T). An overview of the NETS for administrators (NETS-A) is beyond the scope of this book.

National Educational Technology Standards for Students

Technology must be incorporated into the educational environment as both a tool for learning and as a resource if teachers are to prepare students to successfully meet the challenges of the future. Students must be able to select appropriate technological tools that allow them to obtain, analyze, and synthesize information in order to make informed decisions and meet curriculum standards. The NETS project developed the NETS-S to provide teachers with guidelines as to what students (grades PK-12) should know about and be able to do with technology as a tool for learning.

The NETS-S are articulated into six standards that provide performance indicators of what students should know and be able to demonstrate when using technology (see Table 3.1). They define the fundamental concepts, knowledge, skills, and attitudes that students need in order to apply technology in the educational setting. Grade-level performance profiles identify what students should be able to do and know with regard to technology. These profiles provide sequential, age-appropriate activities based on the development of fine motor skills, cognitive ability, and grade level readiness. The NETS-S and the performance profiles serve as guidelines for teachers to use in planning technology enriched lessons that will help their students become technology literate individuals.

It is important to remember that technology is merely a tool to be used to support learning. Learning to use technology should not be the sole focus of a lesson. The technology-enriched lessons should enhance learning of curriculum content as well. For example, in physical education, students can demonstrate their ability to master several NETS-S and NASPE curriculum standards by using heart rate monitors to collect personal heart rate data. After participating in the activity and collecting the data, the students transfer the data to a software program that allows them to use graphing software to develop class intensity profiles.

In this example, students are using technology–the heart rate monitor and the software–in a "real-world" application to collect, analyze, and present data. They are learning about the function of the heart during different types of exercises as well as learning how to apply technology in a physical activity setting. Also, they are meeting the following NASPE standards:

> Standard 1–demonstrating competency in many movement forms in order to participate in the activities.

> Standard 4–achieving and maintaining a health-enhancing level of physical activity by participating in the activity and maintaining their heart rates in the target zones.

The students are also meeting the following NETS-S:

> Standard 1.B–becoming proficient in the use of the heart rate monitors.

> Standard 5.A–using technology to collect data on their heart rates and analyzing the data to improve performance.

By aligning physical activities to meet the NETS-S and the NASPE content standards, students can begin to understand the advantages of using technology to promote and enhance learning. Mitchell, McKethan, & Mohnsen (in press) are developing a text that aligns the NASPE content standards with the NETS-S. This publication will not only align the standards but it will also provide lesson plans for physical educators that incorporate the use of technology into the classroom.

Table 3.1: National Educational Technology Standards for Students

Standard Categories	Performance Indicators
1. Basic operations and concepts	A. Students demonstrate a sound understanding of the concepts operation of technology. B. Students are proficient in the use of technology.
2. Social, ethical, and human issues	A. Students understand the ethical, cultural, and societal issues related to technology. B. Students practice responsible use of technology systems, information, and software. C. Students develop positive attitudes toward technology uses that support lifelong learning, collaboration, personal pursuits, and productivity.
3. Technology productivity tools	A. Students use technology tools to enhance learning, increase productivity, and promote creativity. B. Students use productivity tools to collaborate in producing technology-enhanced models, preparing publications, and producing other creative works.
4. Technology communication tools	A. Students use telecommunications to collaborate, publish, and interact with peers, experts, and other audiences. B. Students use a variety of media and formats to communicate information and ideas effectively to multiple audiences.
5. Technology research tools	A. Students use technology to locate, evaluate, and collect information from a variety of sources. B. Students use technology tools to process data and report results. C. Students evaluate and select new information resources and technological innovations based on the appropriateness to specific tasks.
6. Technology problem-solving and decision-making tools	A. Students use technology resources for solving problems and making informed decisions. B. Students employ technology in the development of strategies for solving problems in the real world.

National Educational Technology Standards for Teachers

NETS-T standards focus on the fundamental concepts, knowledge, skills, and attitudes teachers need to successfully implement technology in the educational environment. NETS-T consists of a comprehensive set of performance-based technology standards and performance indicators for preservice and inservice teachers (see Table 3.2).

Table 3.2: National Educational Technology Standards for Teachers

Standards	Performance Indicators
I. Technology operations and concepts Teachers demonstrate a sound understanding of technology operations and concepts.	A. Teachers demonstrate introductory knowledge, skills, and understanding of concepts related to technology. B. Teachers demonstrate continual growth in technology knowledge and skills to stay abreast of current and emerging technologies.
II. Planning and designing learning environments and experiences Teachers plan and design effective learning environments and experiences supported by technology.	A. Teachers design developmentally appropriate learning opportunities that apply technology-enhanced instructional strategies to support the diverse needs of learners. B. Teachers apply current research on teaching and learning with technology when planning learning environments and experiences. C. Teachers identify and locate technology resources and evaluate them for accuracy and suitability. D. Teachers plan for the management of technology resources within the context of learning activities. E. Teachers plan strategies to manage student learning in a technology-enhanced environment.
III. Teaching, learning, and the curriculum Teachers implement curriculum plans that include methods and strategies for applying technology to maximize student learning.	A. Teachers facilitate technology-enhanced experiences that address content standards and student technology standards. B. Teachers use technology to support learner-centered strategies that address the diverse needs of students. C. Teachers apply technology to develop students' higher-order skills and creativity. D. Teachers manage student learning activities in a technology-enhanced environment.

Table 3.2: National Educational Technology Standards for Teachers

Standards	Performance Indicators
IV. Assessment and evaluation Teachers apply technology to facilitate a variety of effective assessment and evaluation strategies.	A. Teachers apply technology in assessing student learning of subject matter using a variety of assessment techniques. B. Teachers use technology resources to collect and analyze data, interpret results, and communicate findings to improve instructional practice and maximize student learning. C. Teachers apply multiple methods of evaluation to determine students' appropriate use of technology resources for learning, communication, and productivity.
V. Productivity and professional practice Teachers use technology to enhance their productivity and professional practice.	A. Teachers use technology resources to engage in ongoing professional development and lifelong learning. B. Teachers continually evaluate and reflect on professional practice to make informed decisions regarding the use of technology in support of student learning. C. Teachers apply technology to increase productivity. D. Teachers use technology to communicate and collaborate with peers, parents, and the larger community in order to nurture student learning.
VI. Social, ethical, legal, and human issues Teachers understand the social, ethical, legal, and human issues surrounding the use of technology in PK-12 schools and apply that understanding in practice.	A. Teachers model and teach legal and ethical practice related to technology use. B. Teachers apply technology resources to enable and empower learners with diverse backgrounds, characteristics, and abilities. C. Teachers identify and use technology resources that affirm diversity. D. Teachers promote safe and healthy use of technology resources. E. Teachers facilitate equitable access to technology resources for all students.

These standards reflect the skills and knowledge necessary to use technology in support of teaching and learning in the classroom/gymnasium. The overall objective of NETS-T is not simply for teachers to become proficient in using technology, but they also must be able to select appropriate technological tools to use in the educational environment. The NETS-T standards are described in the following sections.

Standard I: Technology Operations and Concepts

Preservice teachers must have the knowledge and skills to use technology efficiently. They will need to continue to improve their technological skills and be knowledgeable of new technologies that they can incorporate into the educational environment.

Standard II: Planning and Designing Learning Environments and Experiences

According to this standard, preservice teachers need to plan and design educational environments that are supported by technologies. Preservice teachers also need to develop management strategies in order to successfully implement technologies in the classroom environment.

Standard III: Teaching, Learning, and the Curriculum

Not only should preservice teachers plan and design lessons using technologies and incorporate technology into the educational environment, they also should teach students to use and apply technology to develop higher order thinking skills and creativity. This standard focuses on the preservice teacher implementing technology-enhanced lessons in a classroom setting, managing the students in this environment, and using technology to support student learning.

Standard IV: Assessment and Evaluation

According to this standard, preservice teachers should be able to apply technology in the assessment of student performance. Preservice teachers also should assess their students' appropriate use of technologies in the classroom.

Standard V: Productivity and Professional Practice

This standard relates directly to the preservice teacher becoming a reflective practitioner. The preservice teacher should use technologies to collaborate, evaluate, and engage in ongoing professional development opportunities. The preservice teacher also should use technologies to increase productivity and communicate with peers, parents, students, and community members to enhance student learning. Technology allows the preservice teacher to readily access new information and stay abreast of current developments in the field of physical education.

Standard VI: Social, Ethical, Legal, and Human Issues

Preservice teachers should model and teach the ethical, legal, and safe uses of technologies, including the risks associated with publishing information on the Internet and the confidentiality of personal data and information. This standard also focuses on identifying and using technologies to affirm student diversity, including locating websites that provide information on children with disabilities or children for whom English is a second language (ESL). Preservice teachers can use such information to provide better service to their students.

NETS-T Performance Profiles

Just as the NETS-S included developmentally appropriate performance profiles for students upon the completion of various grade levels, NETS-T (2002) includes developmentally appropriate performance profiles that describe the technological skills and knowledge preservice teachers should have at various stages in the teacher preparation program. Four sets of performance profiles serve as guidelines for use in developing benchmarks for the preparation and development of technology-literate teachers. These profiles are based on the typical four phases of a teacher preparation program (general/core requirement phase, professional preparation phase, student teaching/internship phase, and first-year teaching phase). Since the profiles are developmental in nature, they enable the teacher preparation program to emphasize the appropriate technology standard(s) at each phase (ISTE, 2002). The four sets of performance profiles relating to each phase are described in the following sections.

General Preparation Performance Profile.

The General Preparation Performance Profile targets technology capabilities that preservice teachers should have upon completion of their general educational coursework or their core course requirements. During the general education experience, preservice teachers use technology as an integral part of the learning process. This profile addresses all of the standards, but specifically emphasizes the first standard, Technology Operations and Concepts. Upon completion of the general preparation component of the teacher preparation program, preservice teachers should be able to meet the competencies listed in the General Preparation Performance Profile (see Table 3.3).

Table 3.3: General Preparation Performance Profile

The Roman numerals in parenthesis refer to the NETS-T standards aligned to that particular competency. *Upon completion of the general preparation component of their program, prospective teachers:*

1. Demonstrate a sound understanding of the nature and operation of technology systems (I).
2. Demonstrate proficiency in the use of common input and output devices; solve routine hardware and software problems; and make informed choices about technology systems, resources, and services (I).
3. Use technology tools and information resources to increase productivity, promote creativity, and facilitate academic learning (I, III, IV, V).
4. Use content-specific tools to support learning and research (I, III, V).
5. Use technology resources to facilitate higher order and complex thinking skills, including problem solving, critical thinking, informed decision- making, knowledge construction, and creativity (I, III, V).
6. Collaborate in constructing technology-enhanced models, preparing publications, and producing other creative works using productivity tools (I, V).
7. Use technology to locate, evaluate, and collect information from a variety of sources (I, IV, V).
8. Use technology tools to process data and report results (I, III, IV, V).
9. Use technology in the development of strategies for solving problems in the real world (I, III, V).
10. Observe and experience the use of technology in their major field of study (III, V).
11. Use technology tools and resources for managing and communicating information (I, V).
12. Evaluate and select new information resources and technological innovations based on their appropriateness to specific tasks (I, III, IV, V).
13. Use a variety of media and formats, including telecommunications, to collaborate, publish, and interact with peers, experts, and other audiences (I, V).
14. Demonstrate an understanding of the legal, ethical, cultural, and societal issues related to technology (VI).
15. Exhibit positive attitudes toward technology uses that support lifelong learning, collaboration, personal pursuits, and productivity (V, VI).
16. Discuss diversity issues related to electronic media (I, VI).
17. Discuss the health and safety issues related to technology use (VI).

Professional Preparation Performance Profile

The professional preparation phase of a teacher preparation program consists of foundations courses that provide the content knowledge, pedagogical knowledge, and content pedagogical knowledge specific to the discipline. In some institutions, this phase is integrated with the general preparation phase. During the professional preparation phase, preservice teachers are admitted to the school or college of education to pursue their teaching license. The technology standards are emphasized along with the specific discipline standards. Specifically, the Professional Preparation Performance Profile emphasizes the second standard, Planning and Designing Learning Environments and Experiences. Upon completion of their preparation coursework and prior to the student teaching or internship experience, preservice teachers should be able to meet the competencies described in the Professional Preparation Performance Profile (see Table 3.4).

Table 3.4: Professional Preparation Performance Profile

The Roman Numerals in parenthesis identify the NETS-T standard(s) addressed by the competency.
Prior to the culminating student teaching or internship experience, prospective teachers:

1. Identify the benefits of technology to maximize student learning and facilitate higher= order thinking skills (I, III).
2. Differentiate between appropriate and inappropriate uses of technology for teaching and learning while using electronic resources to design and implement learning activities (II, III, V, VI).
3. Identify technology resources available in schools and analyze how access-to those resources affects planning for instruction (I, II).
4. Identify, select, and use hardware and software technology resources specially designed for use by PK-12 students to meet specific teaching and learning objectives (I, II).
5. Plan for the management of electronic instructional resources within a lesson design by identifying potential problems and planning for solutions (II).
6. Identify specific technology applications and resources that maximize student learning, address learner needs, and affirm diversity (III, VI).
7. Design and teach technology-enriched learning activities that connect content standards with student technology standards and meet the diverse needs of students (II, III, IV, VI).
8. Design and peer teach a lesson that meets content area standards and reflects the current best practices in teaching and learning with technology (II, III).
9. Plan and teach student-centered learning activities and lessons in which students apply technology tools and resources (II, III).
10. Research and evaluate the accuracy, relevance, appropriateness, comprehensiveness, and bias of electronic information resources to be used by students (II, IV, V, VI).
11. Discuss technology-based assessment and evaluation strategies (IV).
12. Examine multiple strategies for evaluating technology-based student products and the processes used to create those products (IV).
13. Examine technology tools used to collect, analyze, interpret, represent, and communicate student performance data (I, IV).
14. Integrate technology-based assessment strategies and tools into plans for evaluating specific learning activities (IV).
15. Develop a portfolio of technology-based products from coursework, including the related assessment tools (IV, V).
16. Identify and engage in technology-based opportunities for professional education and lifelong learning, including the use of distance education (V).
17. Apply online and other technology resources to support problem solving and related decision making for maximizing student learning (III, V).
18. Participate in online professional collaborations with peers and experts (III, V).
19. Use technology productivity tools to complete required professional tasks (V).
20. Identify technology-related legal and ethical issues, including copyright, privacy, and security of technology systems, data, and information (VI).
21. Examine acceptable use policies for the use of technology in schools, including strategies for addressing threats to security of technology systems, data, and information (VI).
22. Identify issues related to equitable access to technology in school, community, and home environments (VI).
23. Identify safety and health issues related to technology use in schools (VI).
24. Identify and use assistive technologies to meet the special physical needs of students (VI).

Student Teaching/Internship Performance Profile

The culminating student teaching experience is the point when theory becomes practice in real classroom/gymnasium settings. The student teaching phase of the teacher preparation program focuses on applying and integrating theory into practice. The NETS-T student teaching performance profile completes the teaching/learning cycle in that the preservice teachers must implement technology in the planning phase of teaching (Standard II), the actual teaching episode (Standard III), and the assessment of their performance (Standard IV). Upon completion of the culminating student teaching experience, preservice teachers should be able to meet the competencies described in the Student Teaching/Internship Performance Profile (see Table 3.5).

Table 3.5: Student Teaching/Internship Performance Profile

The Roman numerals in parenthesis identify the NETS-T standard(s) addressed by the competency. *Upon completion of the culminating student teaching or internship experience, and at the point of initial licensure, teachers:*

1. Apply troubleshooting strategies for solving routine hardware and software problems that occur in the classroom (I).
2. Identify, evaluate, and select specific technology resources available at the school site and district level to support a coherent lesson sequence (II, III).
3. Design, manage, and facilitate learning experiences using technology that affirms diversity and provides equitable access to resources (II, VI).
4. Create and implement a well-organized plan to manage available technology resources, provide equitable access for all students, and enhance learning competencies (II, III).
5. Design and facilitate learning experiences that use assistive technologies to meet the special physical needs of students (II, III).
6. Design and teach a coherent sequence of learning activities that integrates appropriate use of technology resources to enhance student academic achievement and technology proficiency by connecting district, state, and national curriculum standards with student technology standards (II, III).
7. Design, implement, and assess learner-centered lessons that are based on the current best practices on teaching and learning with technology and that engages, motivates, and encourages self-directed student learning (II, III, IV, V).
8. Guide collaborative learning activities in which students use technology resources to solve authentic problems in the subject area (s) (III).
9. Develop and use criteria for ongoing assessment of technology-based student products and the processes used to create those products (IV).
10. Design an evaluation plan that applies multiple measures and flexible assessment strategies to determine students' technology proficiency and content area learning (IV).
11. Use multiple measures to analyze instructional practices that employ technology to improve planning, instruction, and management (II, III, IV).
12. Apply technology productivity tools and resources to collect, analyze, and interpret data and to report results to parents and students (III, IV).
13. Select and apply suitable productivity tools to complete educational and professional tasks (II, III, V).
14. Model safe and responsible use of technology and develop classroom procedures to implement school and district technology acceptable use policies and data security plans (V, VI).
15. Participate in online professional collaboration with peers and experts as part of a personally designed plan, based on self-assessment, for professional growth in technology (V).

First-Year Teaching Performance Profile

The First-year Teaching Performance Profile presents the technology competencies new teachers should have upon completion of their first year of teaching (see Table 3.6). The technology tasks identified in this profile provide the new teacher, and even the continuing teacher, with ideas for integrating technology into their curriculum, instruction, and assessment. This profile also completes the teaching/learning cycle by having the teachers plan for technology, implement technology into their teaching, and use technology to assess their students.

Table 3.6: First-Year Teaching Performance Profile

The Roman numerals in parenthesis identify the NETS-T standard(s) addressed by the competency. *Upon completion of the first year of teaching, teachers:*

1. Assess the availability of technology resources at the school site, plan activities that integrate available resources, and develop a method for obtaining the additional necessary software and hardware to support the specific learning needs of students in the classroom (I, II, IV).
2. Make appropriate choices about technology systems, resources, and services that are aligned with district and state standards (I, II).
3. Arrange equitable access to appropriate technology resources that enable students to engage successfully in learning activities across subject/content areas and grade levels (II, III, VI).
4. Engage in ongoing planning of lesson sequences that effectively integrate technology resources and are consistent with current best practices for integrating the learning of subject matter and student technology standards (II, III).
5. Plan and implement technology-based learning activities that promote student engagement in analysis, synthesis, interpretation, and creation of original products (II, III).
6. Plan for, implement, and evaluate the management of student use of technology resources as part of classroom operations and in specialized instructional situations (I, II, III, IV).
7. Implement a variety of instructional technology strategies and grouping strategies that include appropriate embedded assessment for meeting the diverse needs of learners (III, IV).
8. Facilitate student access to school and community resources that provide technological and discipline-specific expertise (III).
9. Teach students methods and strategies to assess the validity and reliability of information gathered through technological means (II, IV).
10. Recognize students' talents in the use of technology and provide them with opportunities to share their expertise with their teachers, peers, and others (II, III, V).
11. Guide students in applying self- and peer-assessment tools to critique student= created technology products and the process used to create those products (IV).
12. Facilitate students' use of technology that addresses social needs and cultural identity and promotes interaction with the global community (III, VI).
13. Use results from assessment measures to improve instructional planning, management, and implementation of learning strategies (II, IV).
14. Use technology tools to collect, analyze, interpret, represent, and communicate data for the purposes of instructional planning and school improvement (IV).
15. Use technology resources to facilitate communication with parents or guardians of students (V).
16. Identify capabilities and limitations of current and emerging technology resources and assess the potential of these systems and services to address personal lifelong learning and workplace needs (I, IV, V).

(cont.)

Table 3.6: First–Year Teaching Performance Profile (cont.)

17. Participate in technology-based collaboration as part of continual and comprehensive professional growth to stay abreast of new and emerging technology resources that support enhanced learning for PK–12 student's (V).
18. Demonstrate and advocate for legal and ethical behaviors among students, colleagues, and community members regarding the use of technology and information (V, VI).
19. Enforce classroom procedures that guide students' safe and healthy use of technology and comply with legal and professional responsibilities for students who need assistive technologies (VI).
20. Advocate for equal access to technology for all students in their schools, communities, and homes (VI).
21. Implement procedures consistent with district and school policies that protect the privacy and security of student data and information (VI).

Reprinted with permission from the National Education Technology Standards, ©2002, ISTE (International Society for Technology in Education), 800.336.5191 (U.S. & Canada) or 541.302.3777 (Int'l), iste@iste.org, www.iste.org. All rights reserved. Permission does not constitute an endorsement by ISTE. For more information about the NETS Project, contact Lajeane Thomas, Director, NETS Project, 318.257.3923, lthomas@latech.edu.

Summary

The use of technology in the schooling process helps students achieve important technological capabilities that are essential to their survival in our technology-oriented society. Teachers must be prepared to provide technology-supported learning opportunities, inform students of the advantages of being technology-literate, and empower students to use technology in their lives.

In addition to developing technology-literate students, becoming technology-literate has become a necessity for license renewal and program accreditation. The NETS have been adopted by the National Council for Accreditation of Teacher Education and are now used in evaluating teacher preparation programs for accreditation (NCATE, 2001).

Many state departments of education also have adopted the NETS-S or the NETS-T or both as integral components of teacher license renewal and student graduation requirements. For a complete list of the states that have adopted or at least referenced these standards, visit http://www.cnets.iste.org for a link to a chart of states.

References

International Society for Technology in Education. (1998). *National education technology standards for students.* Eugene, OR: ISTE.

International Society for Technology in Education. (2000). *National education technology standards for teachers.* Eugene, OR: ISTE.

International Society for Technology in Education. (2002). *National education technology standards for administrators.* Eugene, OR: ISTE.

International Society for Technology in Education. (2002). *National education technology standards for teachers: Preparing teachers to use technology.* Eugene, OR: ISTE.

Mitchell, M., McKethan, R., & Mohnsen, B. (in Press). *Integrating technology and learning in physical education.* Cerritos, CA: Bonnie's Fitware.

National Council for Accreditation of Teacher Education. (2001). *Professional standards for the accreditation of schools, colleges, and departments of education.* Washington, DC: NCATE.

Chapter 4
Aligning NASPE/NCATE
BTS and NETS-T

It is difficult to separate technology from the teaching process, teacher behaviors, and student behaviors. In Chapter 1, technology was defined as "...processes in which human beings engage themselves in order to increase control of the material environment" (Anglin, 1995). This definition suggests that technology is intricately infused in our world.

We use technology to communicate, prepare food, move from place to place, diagnose illnesses, entertainment, learn, etc. In a sense, technology (all types) is inseparable from the environment and our experiences within that environment. Physical education and physical activity represent one aspect of the life experience. Consequently, physical education is no different from the total life experience...technology is infused in it, and we are dependent upon it.

It is important for physical educators to pursue instruction based on identified learning competencies, as is the practice in other curricular areas. As a part of the pursuit of identified learning competencies, physical educators also must be intentional about using standard educational technology to support students' acquisition of learning. Failure to do so will support the perception that little or no instruction takes place in physical education.

Regardless of what we teach or don't teach preservice teachers, they will enter a work world that is increasingly dependent upon technologies of all types. It is important that we provide preservice instruction that is relevant. In order for students to consider their physical education experiences as relevant, those experiences must use technology to reflect the real world. Teacher educators with a real world disposition help students see how technology is used in various settings, including physical education. Use of technology in physical education provides students with the tools and competencies to manage their lives, including opportunities for physical activity.

Modeling

Teacher educators must model the use of technology if we expect preservice teachers to value technology. Students often come into teacher education programs with the idea that physical education as a venue is devoid of technology. (Of course, students also often perceive "technology" to be exclusively computer-related technology).

In addition, those who have little experience using technology may view technology operations as being beyond their intellectual capability. Consequently, it becomes imperative that physical education teacher educators model the use of technology in

1. (1) planning,
2. (2) communication,
3. (3) the process of teaching,
4. (4) advocating physical activity, and
5. (5) understanding the need for physical activity.

The systematic use of the National Educational Technology Standards for Teachers (NETS-T) and the NASPE/NCATE Beginning Teacher Standards (NASPE/NCATE BTS) in instructional activities communicates to the preservice teacher that both sets of competencies are essential to student learning and that they are valued by those who deliver instruction in teacher education programs. The following sections show how teacher educators can systematically model both sets of standards in teacher education instructional practices.

Planning: Preservice teachers often come into the teacher education program instilled with dispositions acquired from teachers who failed to recognize the value of planning and/or who delivered programs that were not based on systematic learning competencies. Teacher educators can demonstrate planning competencies that utilize technology resources to identify curriculum and content standards, ways to identify skill progressions and applications, ways in which learning can be individualized to accommodate diverse learners, and ways in which to develop assessment for learning competencies. Physical educators also can use technology to streamline the planning process–developing and using of forms for writing lesson and unit plans, for example.

Communication: Communication addresses activities ranging from sharing information with students to advocacy. Teacher educators must utilize electronic mail in interactions with students, not only to communicate, but also to ensure that students recognize its value. Teacher education professionals must present students with opportunities to collaborate within the class environment and via Internet chat rooms or electronic discussion boards.

The Teaching Process: In modeling teaching, logic would suggest that we cannot operate on the premise that. "Do as I say and not as I do," will somehow deliver the necessary competencies and dispositions that will enable preservice teachers to begin teaching with minimum standards. Consequently, we must not only model the appropriate use of methodological tools but we also must model the appropriate technical, software, and didactic tools. The use of readily available tools gives preservice teachers instructional experiences that, perhaps, they did not have as PK-12 students.

Advocating Physical Activity: The increase of risk factors such as obesity, high blood pressure, and high cholesterol levels among students lends importance to advocacy activities by inservice and preservice teachers. Teachers must have opportunities to advocate by participating in community-based initiatives, writing letters to local newspaper editors, speaking to local civic groups, and delivering in-class presentations. Technology supports advocacy efforts by facilitating collaboration, the location of data, the creation of materials for presentations, and the provision of means for making presentations. Didactic tools such as blood pressure cuffs, stethoscopes, sit-and-reach boxes, and body composition calculators support a hands-on type of learning for not only PK-12 students, but also for parents and community members.

Understanding the Need for Physical Activity: Providing preservice teachers with opportunities to interact with PK-12 students allows for authentic experiences that facilitate an understanding of the need for physical activity. Opportunities to use didactic tools in working with local physical educators and classroom teachers provide preservice teachers with valuable experience. Certainly, examination of data from different perspectives supports and facilitates an understanding of the value of physical activity.

It is important that teacher education programs identify teaching behaviors and technology competencies of beginning teachers. It is equally essential that teachers systematically teach these competencies in their physical education teacher education programs. To systematically address the NASPE/NCATE BTS and NETS-T, lessons must be prefaced with a discussion of their relationship to these two sets of standards. In a sense, these standards should serve as the learning competencies for preservice teachers' instructional experiences.

Technology must be used to support the learning process. It is a tool that, when combined with teacher behaviors and classroom processes, presents an alternative for addressing the myriad of learning styles found in any given class. The integration of technology as a part of learning provides opportunities to internalize learning competencies. The following examples illustrate this assertion:

1) Students in the primary grades may participate in a fitness lesson to learn about the function of the heart. Following vigorous activity, students can place their hands over their chest to feel their heart. Allowing students to use stethoscopes provides an additional experience that supports the learning objective.

2) Fifth grade students participating in a lesson on the overhand throw view the teacher's model of the throw. In the demonstration, students view the major parts of the throw and then see the entire skill modeled. Students participate in tasks and application activities to acquire proper form. The teacher may add video of student performance as a focusing mechanism.

3) In a middle school sport education lesson, student leaders explain the fitness tasks. The teacher incorporates the use of digital photographs to support student understanding and successful performance of the tasks.

The use of technology, when combined with teacher behaviors and class processes, provides another dimension to the teachers' toolbox of strategies to support learning.

Each day, teachers perform tasks that can be supported by technology. Administrative tasks include taking attendance, communicating with parents, requesting or ordering supplies and equipment, recording grades, collecting information about student performance, creating lesson plans, maintaining a discipline file, and setting up tournament brackets for the lunchtime intramural sports program. These tasks can be supported by such technologies as (1) email, (2) handheld computers, (3) databases, (4) electronic grade books, and (5) software designed to create tournament brackets. Although the use of these technologies may not create a "paperless" work environment, it does support efficiency. For example, the use of a database to store student performance data allows the teacher to disaggregate those data. This means that the teacher may identify learning cues that need additional attention or identify those students who need extension tasks that involve greater levels of complexity. Preservice teachers need to understand how technology can support the performance of noninstructional tasks.

Physical educators often are faced with logistical obstacles that are not found in "academic" classrooms. Yet, the local school district charges the physical educator with the same mission as classroom teachers: to provide meaningful instruction with identified learning competencies. The district policies and the building administrator expect physical educators to maintain the same behavioral standards that are found in the classroom setting. Contextual obstacles to meeting these expectations include large teacher-to-student ratios, class schedules with little or no planning time, and class schedules with little or no time between classes.

Technology is a tool that can support both curriculum administration and efficient delivery of instruction. Teacher education instructional experiences often present ideal rather than authentic experiences. These experiences should address how teachers can cope with difficult scheduling, large class sizes, and the lack of time between classes. Consequently, it is important for teacher educators to demonstrate ways in which technology can support lesson preparation, delivery, collection of information about student performances, and analysis of that information to support subsequent instruction.

NASPE/NCATE and NETS-T

This chapter looks at the alignment of the NASPE/NCATE BTS and the NETS-T. The charts in this section identify each NASPE/NCATE BTS (and competencies) and connect to the related NETS-T (and competencies). They are intended to help teacher educators design and model experiences in which the teaching process is related to technology standards. Suggested learning applications that are supported by standards and competencies also are featured. Learning applications that appear in bold face are supported by lesson plans in Chapter 5.

NASPE/NCATE BTS
Standard 1: Content Knowledge

Physical education teachers understand physical education content and disciplinary concepts related to the development of a physically educated person.

NASPE/NCATE BTS	NETS-T	Learning Applications
1.1: Identify critical elements of motor skill performance and combine motor skills into appropriate sequences for the purpose of improving learning.	II. Planning and Designing Learning Environments and Experiences A. Design developmentally appropriate learning opportunities that apply technology-enhanced instructional strategies to support the diverse needs of learners. III. Teaching, Learning, and the Curriculum B. Use technology to support learner-centered strategies that address the diverse needs of students.	Peer video analysis of skills. Word process appropriate skill sequences. Use clip art or Internet art to represent cues for each identified skill element. Examine Internet lesson plans, appropriate sequences, and modifications necessary to meet learning diversity.
1.2: Demonstrate competent motor skill performance in a variety of physical activities.	I. Technology Operations and Concepts: B. Demonstrate continual growth in technology knowledge and skills to stay abreast of current and emerging technologies.	Use digital cameras and camcorders to analyze skill performance of the preservice teacher. Use flat file handheld database to collect information about skill performances.

NASPE/NCATE BTS
Standard 1: Content Knowledge

Physical education teachers understand physical education content and disciplinary concepts related to the development of a physically educated person.

NASPE/NCATE BTS	NETS–T	Learning Applications
1.3: Describe performance concepts and strategies related to skillful movement and physical activity.	III. Teaching, Learning, and the Curriculum B. Use technology to support learner-centered strategies that address the diverse needs of students. D. Manage student learning activities in a technology-enhanced environment. IV. Assessment and evaluation A. Apply technology in assessing student learning of subject matter using a variety of assessment techniques.	Use digital cameras to analyze captured skill sequences. Use the Internet to identify movement characteristics associated with identified disabling conditions. Set up online quizzes, case-based discussions via chat rooms. Use email to communicate with practicing adapted physical educators and regular physical educators. Develop a database of skills with characteristics for each level of proficiencies.
1.4: Describe and apply bioscience and psychological concepts to skillful movement, physical activity, and fitness.	I. Technology Operations and Concepts A. Demonstrate introductory knowledge, skills and understanding of concepts related to technology. II. Planning and Designing Learning Environments and Experiences B. Apply current research on teaching and learning with technology when planning learning environments and experiences.	Use the *FitnessGram* software to examine health related fitness components. Use multimedia instructional software such as the *Body Human* to examine the basis of human movement. Use word processing to develop a goal setting process for personal fitness and skill enhancement.

NASPE/NCATE BTS
Standard 1: Content Knowledge

Physical education teachers understand physical education content and disciplinary concepts related to the development of a physically educated person.

NASPE/NCATE BTS	NETS-T	Learning Applications
1.5: Understand and debate current physical education/activity issues and laws based on historical, philosophical, and sociological perspectives.	II. Planning and Designing Learning Environments and Experiences B. Apply current research on teaching and learning with technology when planning learning environments and experiences. VI. Social, Ethical, Legal, and Human Issues B. Apply technology resources to enable and empower learners with diverse backgrounds, characteristics, and abilities.	Investigate legal issues through Internet sources. Debate curriculum issues (e.g., multi-activity model) via chat room discussions with practicing physical educators. Investigate cultural differences that are found in local school populations by using the Internet to locate ethnic websites. Use information, images in a multimedia presentation on historical development of movement, sports, dance, and teaching practices in physical education.
1.6: Demonstrate knowledge of approved state and national content standards, and local program goals.	I. Technology Operations and Concepts: A. Demonstrate introductory knowledge, skills, and understanding of concepts related to technology. II. Planning and Designing Learning Environments and Experiences C. Identify and locate technology resources and evaluate them for accuracy and suitability. III. Teaching, Learning, and the Curriculum A. Facilitate technology-enhanced experiences that address content standards and student technology standards.	**Use the Internet to locate and align selected state and national physical education standards.** Use the Internet to locate instructional activities and evaluate their suitability using *PE Hall of Shame* articles (Williams, 1989). Create a rubric (using tables in a word processing program) to determine the age-appropriateness of activities by aligning them with state and national standards.

NASPE/NCATE BTS
Standard 2: Growth and Development

Physical education teachers understand how individuals learn and develop and can provide opportunities that support their physical, cognitive, social, and emotional development.

NASPE/NCATE BTS	NETS–T	Learning Applications
2.1: Monitor individual and group performance in order to design safe instruction that meets student developmental needs in the physical, cognitive, and social/emotional domains.	III. Teaching, Learning, and the Curriculum B. Use technology to support learner-centered strategies that address the diverse needs of students. IV. Assessment and evaluation B. Use technology resources to collect and analyze data, interpret results, and communicate findings to improve instructional practice and maximize student learning.	**Videotape lesson at a selected grade level. As a part of the tasks students can complete one or more of the following:** 1. **List and describe any *PE Hall of Shame* elements found in the lesson. Suggest possible changes.** 2. **Examine student success with tasks.** 3. **Examine student use of responsible social behaviors.** 4. **Examine the lesson for teaching behaviors such as (1) Checks for understanding, (2) Teaching by Invitation, and (3) Intra-task variation.**
2.2: Understand the biological, psychological, sociological, experiential, and environmental factors that impact developmental readiness to learn and refine movement skills.	III. Teaching, Learning, and the Curriculum B. Use technology to support learner-centered strategies that address the diverse needs of students. VI. Social, Ethical, Legal, and Human Issues C. Identify and use technology resources that affirm diversity.	Preservice teachers interview a special education teacher or adapted physical education teacher to discuss specific disabilities. Respond to the prompt, "How does the specific disability relate to:" 1. Social behaviors? 2. Level of cognitive functioning? 3. Motor skills? 4. Rate of learning? 5. Are there specific technology tools that support affective, cognitive, or psychomotor learning in physical education?

NASPE/NCATE BTS
Standard 2: Growth and Development

Physical education teachers understand how individuals learn and develop and can provide opportunities that support their physical, cognitive, social, and emotional development.

NASPE/NCATE BTS	NETS-T	Learning Applications

2.3: Identify, select, and implement appropriate learning/practice opportunities based on understanding the student, the learning environment, and the task.	II. Planning and Designing Learning Environments and Experiences
	  A. Design developmentally appropriate learning opportunities that apply technology-enhanced instructional strategies to support the diverse needs of learners.
	V. Productivity and Professional Practice
	  D. Use technology to communicate and collaborate with peers, parents, and the larger community in order to nurture student learning.
		Provide content development experiences for the preservice teacher. Students observe videotaped lesson of two or more grade spans (PK-1; 2-3; 4-5, etc.).
		1. Compare and contrast student performance between grades or grade spans.
		2. Develop content for the skill or skill theme found in the class videos using the content development process identified in *Developing Teaching Skills in Physical Education* (Siedentop & Tannehill, 2000).
		3. Preservice teachers, for informational purposes to parents, post the content development on their website.

NASPE/NCATE BTS
Standard 3: Diverse Students

Physical education teachers understand how individuals differ in their approaches to learning and create appropriate instruction adapted to these differences.

NASPE/NCATE BTS	NETS-T	Learning Applications
3.1: Identify, select, and implement appropriate instruction that is sensitive to students' strengths, weaknesses, multiple needs, learning styles, and prior experiences (e.g. cultural, personal, family, community).	II. Planning and Designing Learning Environments and Experiences B. Apply current research on teaching and learning with technology when planning learning environments and experiences. V. Productivity and Professional Practice D. Use technology to communicate and collaborate with peers, parents, and the larger community in order to nurture student learning.	**Observe (or videotape) a physical education class in a clinical setting. Collect information about student performance using handheld computing devices or laptop computers.** Use information collected from observations of students, sort and categorize the performances using a spreadsheet. Based on the categorized information, develop a word processed lesson plan that accounts for the differences found in the data. Such plans should reflect content analysis, teaching by invitation opportunities, and intra-task variation. Develop a website to provide families and the community with information about grade level health-related fitness data.
3.2: Use appropriate strategies, services, and resources to meet diverse learning needs.	VI. Social, Ethical, Legal, and Human Issues B. Apply technology resources to enable and empower learners with diverse backgrounds, characteristics, and abilities. C. Identify and use technology resources that affirm diversity. E. Facilitate equitable access to technology resources for all students.	Use translation software (or Internet translation sites) to create Spanish equivalent words to English words commonly used in physical education class. Develop task cards that use the translated words to support inclusion of ESL students in physical education. Label technology used by ESL students in physical education.

NASPE/NCATE BTS
Standard 4: Management and Motivation

Physical education teachers understand how individuals differ in their approaches to learning and create appropriate instruction adapted to these differences.

NASPE/NCATE BTS	NETS-T	Learning Applications

4.1: Use managerial routines that create smoothly functioning learning experiences.	II. Planning and Designing Learning Environments and Experiences
	  E. Plan strategies to manage student learning in a technology-enhanced environment.
	V. Productivity and Professional Practice
	  C. Apply technology to increase productivity.
	  D. Use technology to communicate and collaborate with peers, parents, and the larger community in order to nurture student learning.
		Use electronic grade book software (PC, Mac, and PDA) for the maintenance of attendance records.
		Use email to communicate with parents about program events such as fitness testing days, field days, etc.
		Use specialized software such as *Print Master* to print brochures that publicizes special events.
		Maintain student assessment records in a database.
		Develop a website for the purpose of advocating one's physical education program. Include links to supporting organizations such as Centers for Disease Control, American Medical Association, American Heart Association, etc.

4.2: Organize, allocate, and manage resources (e.g., students, time, space, equipment, activities, and teacher attention) to provide active and equitable learning experiences.	II. Planning and Designing Learning Environments and Experiences
	  D. Plan for the management of technology resources within the context of learning activities.
	III. Teaching, Learning, and the Curriculum
	  D. Manage student learning activities in a technology-enhanced environment.
		Develop and maintain a record of program equipment using either a spreadsheet or database program.
		In a station setting, develop a multimedia program to illustrate a skill or concept with which students are working.

NASPE/NCATE BTS
Standard 4: Management and Motivation

Physical education teachers understand how individuals differ in their approaches to learning and create appropriate instruction adapted to these differences.

NASPE/NCATE BTS	NETS–T	Learning Applications
4.2: Organize, allocate, and manage resources (e.g., students, time, space, equipment, activities, and teacher attention) to provide active and equitable learning experiences.	V. Apply Technology to Increase Productivity C. Apply technology to increase productivity. D. Use technology to communicate and collaborate with peers, parents, and the larger community in order to nurture student learning. VI. Social, Ethical, Legal, and Human Issues C. Identify and use technology resources that affirm diversity. E. Facilitate equitable access to technology resources for all students.	Develop a lesson plan file (or activity list) in a word processing file that features the use of bookmarks and hyperlinks to facilitate rapid access to specific lessons or activities. Develop a list of physical activity, wellness, and health-related fitness websites suitable for use by parents and students. Compile a list of technologies (such as amplification devices, laminated task cards, video play back devices) that support student learning. When developing a unit plan, include a list of technology that supports diversity (and inclusion) for disabled students, ESL students, and students who are not disabled or ESL yet come into the classroom with varied ability levels. Develop an instructional unit that features specific plans to equitably use limited technologies in the gym or classroom.

NASPE/NCATE BTS
Standard 4: Management and Motivation

Physical education teachers understand how individuals differ in their approaches to learning and create appropriate instruction adapted to these differences.

NASPE/NCATE BTS	NETS-T	Learning Applications

4.3: Use a variety of developmentally appropriate practices (e.g. content selection, instructional formats, use of music, appropriate incentive/rewards) to motivate students to participate in physical activity inside and outside of the school.	II. Planning and Designing Learning Environments and Experiences
	    E. Plan strategies to manage student learning in a technology-enhanced environment.
	III. Teaching, Learning, and the Curriculum
	    A. Facilitate technology-enhanced experiences that address content standards and student technology standards. Identify and use technology resources that affirm diversity.
	    C. Apply technology to develop students' higher-order skills and creativity.
		Develop a health-related fitness unit that incorporates the use of: (1) metronomes, (2) skinfold calipers, (3) stethoscopes, (4) age appropriate videos, (5) sit and reach boxes and goals, (6) health related fitness websites, (7) computers for students to enter their in-class progress toward health-related fitness.
		Utilize software such as *FitnessGram* or other commercial software for tracking fitness.
		Design and develop a before school, lunchtime or after school intramural program using tournament bracketing software such as *Tournament Builder*.
		Provide preservice teachers with a problem or objective. Develop a unit of study in which students develop an original game (a game that borrows parts of existing games and activities) designed to solve the problem or objective. Preservice teachers present their creation.

NASPE/NCATE BTS
Standard 4: Management and Motivation

Physical education teachers understand how individuals differ in their approaches to learning and create appropriate instruction adapted to these differences.

NASPE/NCATE BTS	NETS–T	Learning Applications
4.4: Use strategies to help students demonstrate responsible personal and social behaviors (e.g., mutual respect, support for others, safety, cooperation) that promote positive relationships and a productive learning environment.	VI. Social, Ethical, Legal, and Human Issues D. Promote safe and healthy use of technology resources.	Develop posters that depict routines to manage classroom processes. Develop a set of posters that address safety considerations for units of study. Develop a set of posters that provide safety cues to be used when students work with various types of physical education equipment.
4.5: Develop an effective behavior management plan.	I. Technology Operations and Concepts A. Demonstrate introductory knowledge, skills, and understanding of concepts related to technology.	Develop a unit of instruction based on Hellison's [1995] *Model for Personal and Social Responsibility* (or other approaches to behavior management). Develop posters (using *PowerPoint* or *Microsoft Publisher*) depicting the outline of the plan for display in the gym. Develop an outline for parents that can be posted on a school website. Assign preservice teachers the task of comparing and contrasting behaviors from selected local boards of education in one or more states.

NASPE/NCATE BTS
Standard 5: Communication

Physical education teachers use knowledge of effective verbal, nonverbal, and media communication techniques to enhance learning and engagement in physical activity settings.

NASPE/NCATE BTS	NETS-T	Learning Applications
5.1: Describe and demonstrate effective communication skills.	VI. Social, Ethical, Legal, and Human Issues D. Promote safe and healthy use of technology resources.	Video analysis of teaching performance evaluating communication skills. Duration recording of talk time, etc. Event recording of the number of times feedback is given, the number of interactions, the number of "ums" or other inappropriate language. Peer transcribing via computer of the lesson.
5.2: Communicate managerial and instructional information in a variety of ways.	II. Planning and Designing Learning Environments and Experiences A. Design developmentally appropriate learning opportunities that apply technology-enhanced instructional strategies to support the diverse needs of learners. E. Plan strategies to manage student learning in a technology-enhanced environment.	Create posters, flyers, and other bulletin board type materials using computers and poster making software, clip art, etc. Create instructional videos to use during class. Create task cards with digital photos inserted into them to explain how to perform the skills on the task cards. Create a musical CD to use as a managerial tool for stopping, starting, changing tempo of movements, etc.

NASPE/NCATE BTS
Standard 5: Communication

Physical education teachers use knowledge of effective verbal, nonverbal, and media communication techniques to enhance learning and engagement in physical activity settings.

NASPE/NCATE BTS	NETS–T	Learning Applications
5.3: Communicate in ways that demonstrate sensitivity to all students.	VI. Social, Ethical, Legal, and Human Issues B. Apply technology resources to enable and empower learners with diverse backgrounds, characteristics, and abilities. C. Identify and use technology resources that affirm diversity.	Analyze the language appropriateness used in classes (being sensitive to gender, race, etc.). Develop task cards that address the skill differences among children (appropriate activities for the GLSP). Develop language cards/physical education dictionary of sign-language or other languages of physical education words used most often. Develop a video along with the cards to teach others the language.
5.4: Describe and implement strategies to enhance communication among students in physical activity settings.	I. Technology Operations and Concepts B. Demonstrate continual growth in technology knowledge and skills to stay abreast of current and emerging technologies. III. Teaching, Learning, and the Curriculum A. Facilitate technology-enhanced experiences that address content standards and student technology standards. IV. Assessment and Evaluation C. Apply multiple methods of evaluation to determine students' appropriate use of technology resources for learning. V. Productivity and Professional Practice D. Use technology to communicate and collaborate with peers, parents, and the larger community in order to nurture students learning.	Develop peer assessment sheets with feedback prompts to prompt students to communicate with one another. Develop peer Internet scavenger hunts in which students must work together to find material on a specific topic.

NASPE/NCATE BTS
Standard 6: Planning and Instruction

Physical education teachers plan and implement a variety of developmentally appropriate instructional strategies to develop physically educated individuals.

NASPE/NCATE BTS	NETS-T	Learning Applications
6.1: Identify, develop, and implement appropriate program and instructional goals. 6.2: Develop long- and short-term plans that are linked to program and instructional goals and student needs.	IV. Assessment and Evaluation B. Use technology resources to collect and analyze data, interpret results, and communicate findings to improve instructional practice and maximize student learning.	Using Internet resources, identify national and state standards that identify what PK-12 students should know and be able to do. Develop a content analysis for a given grade level (or grade span). Use a digital camera to create images for cues that go along with the content analysis. Find and use clipart that accurately depicts learning cues.

6.3: Select and implement instructional strategies, based on selected content, student needs, and safety issues, to facilitate learning in the physical activity setting.	IV. Assessment and Evaluation
	  A. Apply technology in assessing student learning of subject matter using a variety of assessment techniques.
	  B. Use technology resources to collect and analyze data, interpret results, and communicate findings to improve instructional practice and maximize student learning.
		After permission is obtained, observe and videotape a PK-12 lesson in physical education. Examine the videotape to (1) assess student on-task behaviors, (2) examine teacher instructional strategies, (3) note group organization patterns, and (4) identify potential safety issues.
		
		In a peer teaching or clinical teaching setting, use teacher behavior analysis software to obtain event and duration recordings of selected teacher behaviors. Evaluate the data using research findings in teaching as well as the NASPE/NCATE and NET-S competencies for preservice teachers.

NASPE/NCATE BTS
Standard 6: Planning and Instruction

Physical education teachers plan and implement a variety of developmentally appropriate instructional strategies to develop physically educated individuals.

NASPE/NCATE BTS	NETS–T	Learning Applications
6.4: Design and implement learning experiences that are safe, appropriate, relevant, and based on principles of effective instruction.	III. Teaching, Learning, and the Curriculum A. Facilitate technology-enhanced experiences that address content standards and student technology standards.	Create a unit of instruction in health-related fitness that utilizes heart-rate monitors and pedometers, stationary bikes, treadmills, rowing machines, stretch bands, and stepper boxes. Cardiovascular activity is based on target heart rates for specified age groups.
6.5: Apply disciplinary and pedagogical knowledge in developing and implementing effective learning environments.	III. Teaching, Learning, and the Curriculum A. Facilitate technology-enhanced experiences that address content standards and student technology standards.	Use pedometers (that account for distance and intensity) to determine the intensity level (moderate, moderate to vigorous, vigorous) of selected activities.
6.6: Provide learning experiences that allow students to integrate knowledge and skills from multiple subject areas.	I. Technology Operations and Concepts B. Demonstrate continual growth in technology knowledge and skills to stay abreast of current and emerging. II. Planning and Designing Learning Environments A. Design developmentally appropriate learning opportunities that apply technology-enhanced instructional strategies to support the diverse needs of learners.	Develop a unit of study that integrates social studies and fitness for a selected grade level. Select a state and "run" from one geographical point to another. PK-12 students would chart their progress on a map downloaded from the Internet. Students study points of interest that coincide with the running route. Preservice teachers also plan for the integration of math by creating spreadsheets on (1) total daily miles, and (2) average daily miles.

NASPE/NCATE BTS
Standard 6: Planning and Instruction

Physical education teachers plan and implement a variety of developmentally appropriate instructional strategies to develop physically educated individuals.

NASPE/NCATE BTS	NETS-T	Learning Applications
6.6: Provide learning experiences that allow students to integrate knowledge and skills from multiple subject areas.	II. Planning and Designing Learning Environments B. Apply current research on teaching and learning with technology when planning learning environments. III. Teaching, Learning, and the Curriculum A. Facilitate technology-enhanced experiences that address content standards and student technology standards. C. Apply technology to develop students' higher order skills and creativity. D. Manage student learning activities in a technology-enhanced environment.	Develop a unit of study that integrates social studies and fitness for a selected grade level. Preservice teachers select a state (or country) and "run" from one geographical point to another. PK-12 students would chart their progress on a map downloaded from the Internet. Students study points of interest that coincide with the running route. Preservice teachers also plan for the integration of math by creating spreadsheets on (1) total daily miles and (2) average daily miles. Variations for this activity include: 1. Identification of games and activities that are indigenous the region or culture. 2. PK-12 students research the culture, games, and nutrition using the Internet. 3. PK-12 students compute the anticipated destination dates (for selected points of interest) based on average daily miles. 4. PK-12 students prepare a *PowerPoint* presentation based on selected topics from the unit.

NASPE/NCATE BTS
Standard 6: Planning and Instruction

Physical education teachers plan and implement a variety of developmentally appropriate instructional strategies to develop physically educated individuals.

NASPE/NCATE BTS	NETS–T	Learning Applications
6.7: Select and implement appropriate (i.e., comprehensive, accurate, useful, safe) teaching resources and curriculum materials.	II. Planning and Designing Learning Environments C. Apply current research on teaching and learning with technology when planning learning environments and experiences.	Using a word processing tables feature, develop a rubric based on Williams' *Physical of Education Hall of Shame* article (1989) and evaluate unit plans, lesson plans, games, and activities retrieved from Internet sites. A variation of this activity would require preservice teachers to evaluate using NASPE benchmarks and characteristics for a physically educated person.
6.8: Use effective demonstrations and explanations to link physical activity concepts to appropriate learning experiences.	II. Planning and Designing Learning Environments B. Apply current research on teaching and learning with technology when planning learning environments and experiences.	Obtain data from the Centers for Disease Control or American Heart Association to support the emphasis of physical activity in a physical education program. Plan a unit of instruction on physical activity that includes PK-12 students using technology to create bumper stickers, cartoon strips, *PowerPoint* presentations, or letters-to-the editor in support of physical activity.

NASPE/NCATE BTS
Standard 6: Planning and Instruction

Physical education teachers plan and implement a variety of developmentally appropriate instructional strategies to develop physically educated individuals.

NASPE/NCATE BTS	NETS-T	Learning Applications
6.9: Develop and use appropriate instructional cues and prompts to facilitate competent motor skill performance.	I. Technology Operations and Concepts A. Demonstrate introductory knowledge, skills, and understanding of concepts related to technology.	Create instructional cues using: 1. Drawing tools in word processing programs. 2. Paint program software. 3. *Poser* software. 4. Digital cameras. 5. Clip art.
6.10: Develop a repertoire of direct and indirect instructional formats to facilitate student learning (e.g., ask questions, pose scenarios, promote problem solving and critical thinking, facilitate factual recall).	III. Teaching, Learning, and the Curriculum A. Facilitate technology-enhanced experiences that address content standards and student technology standards. C. Apply technology to develop students' higher order skills and creativity.	Preservice teachers, in a sport education season, develop roles that place an emphasis on the use of technology: 1. Statistician uses spreadsheet to maintain game play statistics. 2. Fitness trainers use heart rate monitors to examine cardiovascular intensity of the fitness routine. 3. Publicists develop a season program for the culminating event using *PowerPoint.* 4. Publicists word process game results for the student newspaper. 5. Webmasters create a website to show team mascot, results, goals, etc.

NASPE/NCATE BTS
Standard 7: Student Assessment

Physical education teachers understand and use assessment to foster physical, cognitive, and emotional development of students in physical activity.

NASPE/NCATE BTS	NETS–T	Learning Applications

7.1: Identify key components of various types of assessment, describe their appropriate and inappropriate use, and address issues of validity, reliability, and bias.	II. Planning and Designing Learning Environments and Experiences
	    C. Identify and locate technology resources and evaluate them for accuracy and suitability.
	IV. Assessment and Evaluation
	    C. Apply multiple methods of evaluation to determine students' appropriate use of technology resources for learning, communication, and productivity.
		Develop a rubric to evaluate the appropriateness, validity, and reliability of various technologies (i.e., the *FitnessGram*, software programs, multimedia programs, etc.).
		Have students develop rubrics and evaluate the appropriateness of various technologies.

7.2: Use a variety of appropriate authentic and traditional assessment techniques to assess student performance, provide feedback, and communicate student progress.	IV. Assessment and Evaluation
	    A. Apply technology in assessing student learning of subject matter using a variety of assessment techniques.
	    B. Use technology resources to collect and analyze data, interpret results, and communicate findings to improve instructional practice and maximize student learning.
		Develop a rubric to evaluate the appropriateness, validity, and reliability of various technologies (i.e., the *FitnessGram*, software programs, multimedia programs, etc.).
		Have students develop rubrics and evaluate the appropriateness of various technologies.

NASPE/NCATE BTS
Standard 7: Student Assessment

Physical education teachers understand and use assessment to foster physical, cognitive, and emotional development of students in physical activity.

NASPE/NCATE BTS	NETS–T	Learning Applications

7.3: Involve students in self and peer assessment.	I. Technology Operations and Concepts
	  A. Demonstrate introductory knowledge, skills, and understanding of concepts related to technology.
	
	IV. Assessment and Evaluation
	  A. Apply technology in assessing student learning of subject matter using a variety of assessment techniques.
	  B. Use technology resources to collect and analyze data, interpret results, and communicate findings to improve instructional practice and maximize student learning.
		Have students develop peer skill checklists.
		Students use the *FitnessGram/ActivityGram* to enter fitness data into the computer and produce an activity/fitness profile.
		Use observational handheld software to collect data on peer or self-performance. When doing the self-performance, have students watch videos of themselves.
		Have students develop quizzes using testmaker software dealing with the topic/content.
		Have students develop mindmaps/content maps using software such as *Inspiration*.

7.4: Interpret and use performance data to inform curricular and instructional decisions.	III. Teaching, Learning, and the Curriculum
	  A. Facilitate technology-enhanced experiences that address content standards and student technology standards.
	  B. Use technology to support learner-centered strategies that address the diverse needs of students.
	
	IV. Assessment and Evaluation
	  B. Use technology resources to collect and analyze data, interpret results, and communicate findings to improve instructional practice and maximize student learning.
		Observe students and collect data using observational software to determine students' skill level and provide developmentally appropriate activities for individuals.
		Collect fitness data using *FitnessGram*, etc., and use data to help students set goals for future performances.

NASPE/NCATE BTS
Standard 8: Reflection

Physical education teachers are reflective practitioners who evaluate the effects of their actions on others and seek opportunities to grow professionally.

NASPE/NCATE BTS	NETS–T	Learning Applications
8.1: Use a reflective cycle involving description of teaching, justification of the teaching performance, critique of the teaching performance, the setting of teaching goals, and implementation of change.	I. Technology Operations and Concepts A. Demonstrate introductory knowledge, skills, and understanding of concepts related to technology. V. Productivity and Professional Practice A. Use technology resources to engage in ongoing professional development and lifelong learning. B. Continually evaluate and reflect on professional practice to make informed decisions regarding the use of technology in support of student learning.	Word process reflective logs describing teaching episodes, critiquing teaching (strengths/weaknesses), and then setting goals for the next teaching episode. Capture videos of teaching episodes to illustrate teaching performances (strengths and weaknesses). Insert these video segments into the reflective log to justify teaching and pinpoint changes made the next time the lesson is taught.
8.2: Use available resources to develop as a reflective professional.	V. Productivity and Professional Practice A. Use technology resources to engage in ongoing professional development and lifelong learning.	Use chat rooms, listservs, and email to communicate about the profession with others. Participate in continuing education through online courses. Create performance rubrics using rubric-maker software to assess/evaluate teaching performances and communicate with others about what worked. Participate in computer-generated PRAXIS exams.

NASPE/NCATE BTS
Standard 8: Reflection

Physical education teachers are reflective practitioners who evaluate the effects of their actions on others and seek opportunities to grow professionally.

NASPE/NCATE BTS	NETS–T	Learning Applications
8.3: Construct a plan for continued professional growth based on the assessment of personal teaching performance.	V. Productivity and Professional Practice A. Use technology resources to engage in ongoing professional development and lifelong learning. D. Use technology to communicate and collaborate with peers, parents, and the larger community in order to nurture student learning.	Word process a table identifying current status (rating) as a teacher, goals to shoot for, and completion boxes in order to maintain an ongoing professional growth plan. Assess student learning via observational programs, *FitnessGram*, rubrics, etc. Then compile these data using spreadsheet software and graphing software to determine the rate of student learning and make teaching decisions based on that information.

NASPE/NCATE BTS
Standard 9: Technology

Physical education teachers use information technology to enhance learning and to enhance personal and professional productivity.

NASPE/NCATE BTS	NETS–T	Learning Applications
9.1: Demonstrate knowledge of current technologies and their application to physical education.	I. Technology Operations and Concepts 　B. Demonstrate continual growth in knowledge and skills to stay abreast of current and emerging technologies. II. Planning and Designing Learning Environments and Experiences 　B. Apply current research on teaching and learning with technology when planning learning environments and experiences.	Conduct an online search of new technologies and assess their applicability to the field of physical education and teaching. Conduct an online search of research (experimental and action) that has been conducted on various pieces of technology. Using the findings of the research, make more informed decisions about the use of technology in the physical education classroom. Implement technology such as virtual reality, "whole body" video games (e.g., *Dance Dance Revolution*), heart rate monitors, pedometers, handheld computers, and applicable software.

NASPE/NCATE BTS
Standard 9: Technology

Physical education teachers use information technology to enhance learning and to enhance personal and professional productivity.

NASPE/NCATE BTS	NETS-T	Learning Applications

9.2: Design, develop, and implement student learning activities that integrate information technology.	II. Planning and Designing Learning Environments and Experiences
	   A. Design developmentally appropriate learning opportunities that apply technology-enhanced instructional strategies to support the diverse needs of learners.
	   D. Plan for the management of technology resources within the context of learning activities.
	   E. Plan strategies to manage student learning in a technology-enhanced environment.
	III. Teaching, Learning, and the Curriculum
	   A. Facilitate technology-enhanced experiences that address content standards and student technology standards.
	   B. Use technology to support learner-centered strategies that address the diverse needs of students.
	IV. Assessment and Evaluation
	   A. Apply technology in assessing student learning of subject matter using a variety of assessment techniques.
		Develop (word process) a lesson plan/unit plan that incorporates the use of technology in physical education. The plan focuses on the teacher's ability to implement technology into a class with a large number of students. For example, a lesson plan might incorporate the use of technology in a dance unit. The technologies that are used in this plan could range from *Dance Dance Revolution* (video game) in helping with eye-foot coordination and rhythms to heart rate monitors to measure intensity. In order to integrate technology successfully into a class with large numbers (e.g., 35 students) has been an issue. This activity is aimed at helping teachers solve the problem of using technology with large numbers of students. Develop (word process) a sign-in sheet to make sure that equitable access to computers and other types of technology is provided.
		
		Design lessons that incorporate students' using technology to meet the physical education standards.

NASPE/NCATE BTS
Standard 9: Technology

Physical education teachers use information technology to enhance learning and to enhance personal and professional productivity.

NASPE/NCATE BTS	NETS–T	Learning Applications
9.3: Use technology to communicate, network, locate resources, and enhance continuing professional development.	V. Productivity and Professional Practice D. Use technology to communicate and collaborate with peers, parents, and the larger community in order to nurture student learning.	Provide students with experiences that use the following: 1. Networks 2. Emails 3. Listservs 4. Chat Rooms 5. Online Searches 6. Online Courses

NASPE/NCATE BTS
Standard 10: Collaboration

Physical education teachers foster relationships with colleagues, parents/guardians, and community agencies to support students' growth and well-being.

NASPE/NCATE BTS	NETS–T	Learning Applications
10.1: Identify strategies to become an advocate in the school and community to promote a variety of physical activity opportunities.	V. Productivity and Professional Practice D. Use technology to communicate and collaborate with peers, parents, and the larger community in order to nurture student learning.	Develop a checklist of the technology available for use in the school. From this list, develop a list of needs to help facilitate student learning. Communicate with others about the importance of physical education via email and chat rooms. Create a physical education website that provides information about the physical education program, links to other physical education websites, and other materials that advocate the importance of physical education.
10.2: Actively participate in the professional physical education community and within the broader education field.	V. Productivity and Professional Practice A. Use technology resources to engage in ongoing professional development and lifelong learning.	Register online for conferences and events. Join a listserv to receive updated information and to chat with others about physical education material. Take online courses. Develop presentations using technology (e.g., *PowerPoint*) and present at conferences.

NASPE/NCATE BTS
Standard 10: Collaboration

Physical education teachers foster relationships with colleagues, parents/guardians, and community agencies to support students' growth and well-being.

NASPE/NCATE BTS	NETS-T	Learning Applications
10.3: Identify and seek community resources to enhance physical activity opportunities.	V. Productivity and Professional Practice A. Use technology resources to engage in ongoing professional development and lifelong learning. D. Use technology to communicate and collaborate with peers, parents, and the larger community in order to nurture student learning.	Establish links with businesses within the community through telephone, email, flyers, etc., to share information about the importance of physical activity and physical education. Locate local grants using the Internet and public communications personnel, and apply for grants.
10.4: Establish productive relationships with parents/guardians and school colleagues, to support student growth and well-being.	V. Productivity and Professional Practice D. Use technology to communicate and collaborate with peers, parents, and the larger community in order to nurture student learning.	Website development. Create a monthly physical education newsletter. Have students become reporters for the newsletter, reporting on physical education events that are occurring in school, locally, and nationally. Create a physical education Parent Volunteer Day sign-up sheet. Communicate with parents through the newsletter about the importance of becoming involved in their child's school endeavors, including physical education. Parents volunteer to participate in physical activities in their child's physical education class. Have two-three parents daily on a revolving basis. Create a calendar that identifies who will be attending when.

Summary

This chapter illustrated the alignment between NASPE/NCATE BTS and NETS-T. The two sets of standards and competencies have been placed side-by-side to help readers visualize the similarities that exist and to identify learning experiences that connect both sets. The suggested learning experiences are not intended to be exhaustive, but rather to provide a beginning point for the identification of relevant learning experiences. Chapter 5 illustrates selected learning experiences in greater detail.

References

Anglin, E. (1995). *Instructional technology: Past, present, and future* (2nd ed.). Englewood, CO: Libraries Unlimited.

Hellison, D. (1995). *Teaching personal and social responsibility through physical activity.* Champaign, IL: Human Kinetics.

International Society for Technology in Education. (2000). *National education technology standards for teachers.* Eugene, OR: ISTE.

National Association for Sport and Physical Education. (2001). *Standards for initial programs in physical education teacher education.* Reston, VA: Author. Available at: http://www.aahperd.org/naspe/pdf_files/standards_initial.pdf.

Siedentop, D., & Tannehill, D. (2000). *Developing Teaching Skills in Physical Education* (4th ed.) Mountain View, CA: Mayfield Publishing Company.

Williams, N. (1989). The Physical Education Hall of Shame. *Journal of Physical Education, Recreation and Dance, 63,* 57-60.

Chapter 5
Integrating Technology into PETE Programs

The NASPE/NCATE Beginning Teacher Standards (NASPE/NCATE BTS) and the National Educational Technology Standards for Teachers (NETS-T) delineate the knowledge and skills necessary for teachers to be effective. By aligning the NETS-T with the NASPE/NCATE BTS, physical educators are able to become technology-literate, effective teachers who incorporate technology into their daily teaching routines.

This chapter focuses on model learning activities and classroom examples that show how the aligned standards can be met. Each learning activity integrates technology with content that would likely be encountered in the physical education teacher preparation program. It also includes ideas for assessing and evaluating the learning competencies. The focus of the lesson plans is to move beyond the professor's use of a presentation tool to a teacher candidate's experience in learning with technology and creating experiences for students to use technology as a learning tool. This chapter places technology in the hands of learners, creating a learner-centered and inquiry-oriented learning environment.

The lesson plans presented here provide examples of ways to integrate technology into teaching. The examples are not on the "cutting edge." Rather, most of the software and hardware cited can be obtained easily or is already present in most colleges and universities.

Design of the Lesson Plan

The lesson plans are based on the NASPE/NCATE BTS and are aligned to specific NETS-T. The page layout is designed to help the reader see clearly what the expectations are of both the instructor and the teacher candidate.

Reading down a single column will provide only a glimpse of the action that is taking place. Read down and across the columns in each section to gain a full view of what is expected.

The following sections introduce each lesson:

Topic - Highlights the NASPE/NCATE BTS content area of physical education and technology competencies.

Objectives - Learning competencies for the preservice teacher.

Cross-Reference - Highlights the specific NASPE/NCATE BTS and NETS-T application located in Chapter 4's alignment matrix.

Physical Education Equipment Needed - List of equipment that is needed.

Technology Requirements - List of necessary software, hardware, Internet capabilities, etc.

Other Resources - List of necessary articles, books, etc.

Lesson Summary - Provides a brief description of the lesson.

Standards - States both the applicable NASPE/NCATE BTS and performance competencies and the NETS-T and performance competencies.

Lesson Description - Lists what the physical education teacher educator faculty or staff developer should be doing, in the order it should be done. Also outlines the expectations of preservice teachers as the activity takes place. This column provides a check on how involved the candidates should be in the lesson.

Reflection - Highlights the important points of the lesson. Also provides comments about implementing the activities from those who have used them.

The lessons and activities provided in this chapter are templates that can be incorporated in the user's classroom. For this reason, assessment rubrics and evaluation checklists have not been developed for each lesson plan. There are several websites that can provide help in developing rubrics to measure student competencies. They include:

> http://www.teach-nology.com/web_tools/rubrics/

> http://rubistar.4teachers.org/

> http://www.mcasmentor.com/rubrics.htm

Lesson Focus: 1
NASPE/NCATE Standard 1 – Content Knowledge

Topic	Alignment of National Physical Education Standards to National Health Goals
Cross-Reference	NASPE/NCATE Standard 1 - Outcome 1.6
Lesson Objectives	Upon completion of this lesson, the preservice teacher will be able to identify the National Physical Education Content Standards and the Healthy People 2010 goals. The preservice teacher will analyze the documents and align them with one another. The preservice teacher will list physical education activities that could help individuals meet the Healthy People 2010 goals. The preservice teacher will develop a statement of why physical education is important based on these documents.
Lesson Summary	The preservice teacher will locate online the Healthy People 2010 document and the NASPE Content Standards document and will align the two documents, creating a rationale for how physical education can be a tool in the fight against declining health among Amcrica's youth.
PE Equipment Requirements	None

Technology Requirements	Computers with Internet access
	Data projector
	URLs:
	    Healthy People2010: http://www.cdc.gov/nchs/about/otheract/hpdata2010/abouthp.htm
	    NASPE Content Standards: http://www.aahperd.org/naspe/stdspe.html

Other	None

Alignment of Standards: 1

NASPE/NCATE BTS

Standard 1
Content Knowledge
Outcome 1.6
Knowledge of local, state, and national content standards and goals.

Standard 9
Technology
Outcome 9.3
Technological resources and communication.

NETS-T

Standard I
Technology Operations and Concept
Outcome I-A
Introductory knowledge and skills.

Lesson Description: 1

Instructor's Responsibilities & Roles	Preservice Teacher's Responsibilities & Roles
Pre-Instructional Phase	
Assign preservice teachers to locate and retrieve popular media accounts of the current health status of Americans to bring to class. Arrange the class to meet in the computer lab or have access to computers for the lesson's application activity.	Collect popular media accounts of the health status of Americans.
Instructional Phase	
You were to bring in articles and advertisements that you found in popular magazines and journals. Work in small groups of about four people and discuss the material you found. Create a list of any data that are common in the articles and any statistics that are presented. Research demonstrates that being physically active is important to the health and well-being of individuals. There is overwhelming evidence of the role physical activity plays in preventing disease. Exercise and fitness were identified as one of the nation's goals to help prevent disease in the Healthy People 2000 and Healthy People 2010 documents. Documents such as Healthy People 2000 and Healthy People 2010 were used to develop guidelines for health professions, including	Participate in small-group discussion about the articles on the current health status of Americans. As a group, create a list of data that are common throughout the articles and any statistics that are provided. Visit the Healthy People 2010 website at http://www.cdc.gov/nchs/about/otheract/hpdata2010/abouthp.htm.Participate in discussion about Healthy People 2010.

Lesson Description: 1

Instructor's Responsibilities & Roles	Preservice Teacher's Responsibilities & Roles

Instructional Phase

physical educators. The intent was to help promote healthy lifestyles for all people. Please locate the Healthy People 2010 website at this time.

Physical educators have the potential to improve the well-being and health of their students by providing the foundation for being physically, emotionally, socially, and cognitively capable of participating in physical activities in the school environment. A quality physical education program can help students meet the goals and objectives set forth by the Healthy People reports. According to NASPE, the main purpose of physical education is to help students become physically educated individuals who continue to participate in physical activities throughout their lifetime. What is a physically educated person? {Has, Is, Knows, Does, Values} Based on this definition, NASPE developed the seven content standards. These standards identify what a student should know and be able to do as a result of a quality physical education program.

Locate the NASPE content standard document at this time.

Define what a physically educated person is. A physically educated person is a person who:

1. Has learned skills necessary to perform a variety of physical activities.
2. Is physically fit.
3. Participates regularly in physical activity.
4. Knows the implications and benefits of involvement in physical activities.
5. Values physical activity and its contributions to a healthful lifestyle.

Locate NASPE Content Standards document: http://www.aahperd.org/naspe/.

Lesson Description: 1

	Instructor's Responsibilities & Roles	Preservice Teacher's Responsibilities & Roles
Instructional Phase	These two documents are important because they both emphasize the importance of being active and valuing physical activity in order to live a healthy life. Physical education can play a major role in achieving the national goal of being physically fit and active. By creating a developmentally appropriate physical education program and offering daily physical education, physical educators can begin to teach children to appreciate physical activity and enjoy participating in physical activities.	
Application(S)	1. Now that you have located both documents, you are to select one objective from the Healthy People 2010 document. 2. Describe the objective, including activities that may address or help a person obtain that objective. 3. Determine if that objective can be aligned to the NASPE content standards. 4. Describe how that objective is aligned, stating the standards that specifically relate to that objective. 5. Provide a list of activities that can be done in physical education class to help students attain that Healthy People 2010 objective. 6. Develop a rationale that addresses importance of physical education in the public school curriculum.	Complete the assignment individually. 1. Locate *Healthy People 2010* website and select 1 objective. 2. Provide example activities to help students meet the selected objective. 3. Align the objective to the NASPE content standards. 4. Provide reasons for the identified alignments. 5. Identify physical activities that can be concluded in a physical education class. 6. Using *Healthy People 2010* and the NASPE content standards develop a rationale supporting the inclusion of physical education in the curriculum.

Lesson Description: 1

Instructor's Responsibilities & Roles

Preservice Teacher's Responsibilities & Roles

Lesson Closure

Have preservice teachers present their products, allowing time for questions from you and others.

The two documents—Healthy People 2010 and the NASPE Content Standards—can be used to advocate the importance of physical education. By aligning standards and objectives such as these, we can emphasize how physical education activities can help meet national health goals.

Participate in the presentation of the application activity product. Ask and answer questions relevant to the assignment.

Lesson Reflection and Extensions

1. This lesson focused on preservice teachers identifying the established national health goals, Healthy People 2010, and the National Physical Education Content Standards. Preservice teachers engaged in an online search of these documents to locate and synthesize information about how they could be aligned to meet the purpose of improving American's health.
2. This application activity also can be extended to include the alignment of state physical education standards. (Most states have physical education curriculum standards. These standards, which can generally be found on the state department of education website.)
3. This lesson was implemented in an introductory physical education course. The preservice teachers gained knowledge of the standards that existed and were able to state the relationships between the local, state, and national standards. One preservice teacher noted that "this assignment helped me realize the impact physical education could have on the health of American children."

Lesson Focus: 2
NASPE/NCATE Standard 2 – Growth & Development

Topic	Determining the skill levels of students and designing appropriate learning experiences based on assessment.
Cross-Reference	NASPE/NCATE Standard 2 - Outcome 2.1
Lesson Objectives	Upon completion of this lesson, the preservice teacher will assess the developmental skill levels of children in order to plan developmentally appropriate activities for them and promote skill learning. The preservice teacher will develop developmentally appropriate activities based on the individual needs of the children.
Lesson Summary	Preservice teachers will create a rubric to assess the skill levels of children dribbling basketballs. They will observe a small group of children performing the basketball dribble and categorize their performances into one of the four general levels of skill proficiency (pre-control, control, utilization, and proficiency). The preservice teachers will then develop appropriate dribbling activities for each skill level.
PE Equipment Requirements	One basketball for each child. Cones (five per each group of children).
Technology Requirements	Computers Rubric maker software Data projector Internet access (rubric maker) Clip art (for developing cue posters) TV/VCR Video of children at various levels of skill proficiency performing a selected skill
Other	Rubric for assessing children's dribbling skill level Cue posters

Alignment of Standards: 2

NASPE/NCATE BTS

Standard 2
Growth and Development
Outcome 2.1
Monitor individual and group performance in order to design safe instruction that meets student developmental needs in the physical, cognitive, and social/emotional domains.

Standard 3
Diverse Students
Outcome 3.1
Appropriate instruction based on individual student needs.

Standard 6
Planning and Instruction
Outcome 6.4
Design and implement learning experiences that are safe, appropriate, relevant, and based on principles of effective instruction.

Standard 9
Technology
Outcome 9.1
Design, develop, and implement student learning activities that integrate information technology.

NETS-T

Standard 3
Teaching, Learning, and the Curriculum
Outcome III-A
Use technology to support learner-centered strategies that address the diverse needs of students.

Standard 4
Assessment and Evaluation
Outcome IV-B
Use technology resources to collect and analyze data, interpret results, and communicate findings to improve instructional practice and maximize student learning.

Lesson Description: 2

	Instructor's Responsibilities & Roles	Preservice Teacher's Responsibilities & Roles
Pre-Instructional Phase	Locate or develop a video of children at different levels of skill proficiency performing a specific skill. Arrange for preservice teachers to observe elementary school children performing the basketball dribble (or other skill). Arrange for class to have access to computers with Internet access and/or rubric maker software.	
Instructional Phase	In any given class, PK-12, students will enter with various motor abilities, levels of cognitive functioning, and dispositions toward physical activity. The lesson design and the degree to which teachers differentiate instruction (based on content development) impact each of the three learning domains: cognitive, affective, and psychomotor. Content development is important in that it supports progressive and sequential lessons, based on the individual needs of the children. One of your challenges as a teacher is to match the content of your lessons to the abilities of your students, rather than to their age and grade level. Why not just use the age or grade level of the student? [Age or grade level is not an accurate measure of ability. By assessing the student's developmental level, you can then begin to provide developmentally appropriate activities.]	Listen and participate in discussion.

Lesson Description: 2

Instructor's Responsibilities & Roles	Preservice Teacher's Responsibilities & Roles

Instructional Phase

Motor development is usually the focus of one class you will take in your professional preparation curriculum. It specifically addresses the developmental levels of students. What do you think motor development deals with? [It is a highly interrelated process that deals with learning in the three domains, age-related behaviors, and biological or environmental constraints].

What are the three learning domains? [Cognitive, affective, and psychomotor.]

Physical education focuses mainly on the psychomotor domain, the domain of movement. Children enter physical education with many different psychomotor abilities.

Show the General Levels of Skill Proficiency (GLSP) chart. As with cognitive development, physical/skill development progresses in stages. The GLSP chart on the board was developed to help you assess the developmental skill levels of your students. This classification system can serve as a guide not only for assessing the ability levels of your students, but also for helping you to select tasks that match their abilities. Each skill level has observable characteristics to help you identify student abilities.

Describe each section of the chart, including examples of children performing a skill at that level.

Listen and participate in discussion.

Lesson Description: 2

	Instructor's Responsibilities & Roles	Preservice Teacher's Responsibilities & Roles
Application(S)	1. Develop the cues and posters for the basketball dribble that will be taught. 2. Using the rubric maker software or the rubric maker found online, preservice teachers develop a rubric to assess the skill levels of children performing the basketball dribble. 3. Observe children (elementary school) performing the basketball dribble. 4. Assess each child's performance and determine in which category of the GLSP each child falls. 5. Develop a list of developmentally appropriate activities using the Internet to locate activities for children at each GLSP level.	1. Preservice teachers determine the cues for the basketball dribble that will be assessed. Then they will create cue posters, inserting clip art to teach each identified cue. 2. Based on the GLSP chart, preservice teachers will develop a rubric to use when assessing the children practicing the basketball dribble. The rubric should be made using rubric maker software. 3. Observe the children practicing the basketball dribble. 4. Assess the children practicing the basketball dribble and use the rubric to determine each child's level of skill proficiency. 5. Based on the assessment of the children's performances, the preservice teachers will devise developmentally appropriate progressions of activities for children at each level of skill proficiency.
Lesson Closure	Knowledge of students' skill levels will help you plan developmentally appropriate activities for your students so they will experience some degree of success and still be challenged. By knowing the skill abilities of your students, you will be able to individualize instruction in order to facilitate learning.	Be attentive and ask questions.
Lesson Reflection and Extensions	1. This lesson plan focuses on the developmental stages of children's physical abilities. Knowing the developmental levels of children will help preservice teachers plan and individualize appropriate instruction. 2. This lesson focuses on the psychomotor domain and children's readiness to learn.	

Lesson Focus: 3
NASPE/NCATE Standard 3 – Diverse Students

Topic	Students with disabilities in physical education.
Cross-Reference	NASPE/NCATE Standard 3 - Outcome 3.2
Lesson Objectives	Preservice teachers will identify the characteristics of children with certain disabilities. Preservice teachers will develop a list of teaching strategies to include children with those disabilities in the physical education classroom.
Lesson Summary	Preservice teachers will locate information about disabilities on the Internet and create a disability pocket reference based on the information found.
PE Equipment Requirements	None
Technology Requirements	Computers with Internet access Word processor Search engine (i.e., www.google.com) URLs for disabilities
Other	Disability Internet Scavenger Hunt Handout

Alignment of Standards: 3

NASPE/NCATE BTS

Standard 3
Diverse Students
Outcome 3.2
Appropriate resources to meet diverse learning needs.

Standard 9
Technology
Outcome 9.3
Technological resources and communication.

NETS–T

Standard III
Teaching, Learning, and the Curriculum
Outcome III-B
Use technology to support learner-centered strategies that address the diverse needs of students.

Standard VI
Social, Ethical, Legal, and Human Issues
Outcome VI-C
Identify and use technology resources that affirm diversity.

Lesson Description: 3

	Instructor's Responsibilities & Roles	Preservice Teacher's Responsibilities & Roles
Pre-Instructional Phase	Develop the Disability Internet Scavenger Hunt handout. Arrange for the class to have Internet access.	Develop a list of how children in a classroom can differ.
Instructional Phase	Review the lists the preservice teachers compiled. Compose a comprehensive class list on the board. Just as no two snowflakes are exactly alike, no two children are exactly alike. You will have boys and girls in your classes with special needs, with different skill levels, and from various cultures. Every child is different. In order to be an effective physical educator, you will need to design and provide experiences that include all children. Discovering your students' abilities and helping them succeed is critical to helping them becoming physically educated individuals. What are some disabilities that might be evident in some children? Write the answers on the board.	Present ideas and add to the comprehensive class list. Participate in discussion by answering questions.

Lesson Description: 3

	Instructor's Responsibilities & Roles	Preservice Teacher's Responsibilities & Roles
Instructional Phase	What do you think the term "inclusion" means? Inclusion involves educating children with disabilities alongside their non-disabled peers with the use of appropriate supports. Inclusion encompasses the philosophy that all children can learn and all children want to learn. It is not mandated by law, but Public Law 94-142 (Education for All Handicapped Children-1975) and the Individuals with Disabilities Education Act (IDEA) of 1990 guarantee all children with disabilities a free and appropriate education in the least restrictive environment. Through inclusion, the unique abilities of all students, even those without disabilities, are identified and nurtured. Today we're going to focus on including children with special needs.	Participate in discussion by answering questions and posing questions.
Application(S)	1. Introduce the Disability Internet Scavenger Hunt handout. 2. Have preservice teachers complete the handout by locating websites that contain reliable information about the disabilities and answering the questions.	1. Ask any questions regarding the handout. 2. Complete the handout by locating websites that contain information about the disabilities and answering the questions on the handout.

Lesson Description: 3

	Instructor's Responsibilities & Roles	**Preservice Teacher's Responsibilities & Roles**
Application(S)	3. Based on the information found, preservice teachers develop a pocket reference that identifies the typical behaviors/characteristics of the identified disabilities and teaching strategies to successfully include students with those particular disabilities. Disabilities for the pocket reference are visual impairments, hearing impairments, physical disabilities (select two specific disabilities that result in physical conditions), and emotional disturbances.	3. Develop a pocket reference that provides a description of the typical behaviors/characteristics and teaching strategies to successfully include children with those disabilities in your physical education program. The teaching strategies should include any modifications that will need to be made. A. Identify the disability. B. Bulleted list of typical behaviors/ characteristics. C. Bulleted list of teaching strategies including any modifications to the teaching environment and equipment.
Lesson Closure	When children with special needs are included in your program, those children are not the only one who must adjust. The teacher and the other students will need to adjust as well. I have listed a few tips from the trenches on successful inclusion in your program: -Familiarize yourself with the child's disability. -Base your instruction on the student's individual needs and capabilities. -Read and follow the IEP. -Establish a warm and positive learning environment that fosters acceptance of everyone.	Participate in the discussion.

Lesson Description: 3

| Instructor's Responsibilities & Roles | Preservice Teacher's Responsibilities & Roles |

Lesson Closure

Hold the same expectations for all children.

Get to know your students.

Assess the student's capabilities and then provide the necessary instruction.

Foster cooperation and teamwork among the students in your class.

Lesson Reflection and Extensions

1. This lesson plan focuses on the different types of disabilities that children who are included in your physical education program might have.
2. By developing a reference guide with simple modifications and teaching tips, preservice teachers have a tool at their fingertips to help them be more successful in the classroom.

Lesson Focus: 4
NASPE/NCATE Standard 4 – Management & Motivation

Cross-Topic Reference	Establishing structure.
	NASPE/NCATE Standard 4 - Outcome 4.1
Lesson Objectives	Preservice teachers will develop rules and consequences posters.
	Preservice teachers will establish lesson protocols to establish structure.
	Preservice teachers will implement lesson protocols in a teaching situation.
	Preservice teachers will analyze before and after teaching episodes to determine the necessity for lesson protocols, rules, and consequences.
Lesson Summary	Preservice teachers will teach a physical education class before structure is established in the gymnasium. Then, they will establish structure by developing rules, consequences, and lesson protocols. Once these have been established, the preservice teachers will implement them by teaching activities that emphasize and reinforce the rules, consequences, and lesson protocols. Preservice teachers will focus on establishing structure for at least one week. After one week, they will teach the same lesson that was taught before structure was established. Both lessons will be taped and analyzed using the observational software to identify differences in teacher and student behavior.
PE Equipment Requirements	Varies with equipment listed on lesson plans that are developed.
Technology Requirements	Video cameras Computer with word processing software Wireless microphones Observation software CD player Poster maker software Laminating machine
Other	Whistles Music Videotape

Alignment of Standards: 4

NASPE/NCATE BTS

Standard 4
Management and Motivation
Outcome 4.1
Managerial routines.

NETS-T

Standard IV
Assessment and Evaluation
Outcome IV-B
Use technology resources to collect and analyze data, interpret results, and communicate findings to improve instructional practice and maximize student learning.

Lesson Description: 4

	Instructor's Responsibilities & Roles	**Preservice Teacher's Responsibilities & Roles**
Pre-Instructional Phase	Arrange teaching internships for preservice teachers.	Develop and implement a lesson plan that provides developmentally appropriate basketball activities.
	Develop examples of rules and consequences.	Videotape the teaching episode and use observational software to analyze the teaching performance.
Instructional Phase	Review the data analysis from the teaching episodes, identifying reoccurring themes dealing with management issues and talk time.	Participate in discussion.

When you think about teaching physical education, you probably think about one of two things: What am I going to teach? How am I going to manage all those children in a moving environment? For beginning teachers, management and motivation are of great concern. Questions that are often asked by novice teachers are:

-How am I going to get students to do what I want them to do?

-How do I motivate them to learn?

-Will they follow my directions?

-If they don't follow my directions, then what will I do?

Lesson Description: 4

Instructor's Responsibilities & Roles

Preservice Teacher's Responsibilities & Roles

Instructional Phase

-Did any of you have these questions as you prepared for your first teaching lesson?

All of these questions deal with management issues. Management deals with arranging the environment to maximize student learning, and maintaining and developing appropriate behavior and student engagement. Before effective teaching can take place, you must develop good management skills and become an effective manager. You must establish your structure by developing rules, consequences, and lesson protocols. Not only must you establish these things, but you also must teach your students the rules and protocols.

According to Soar & Soar (1979) you need to use the first 14 days of the class to develop, explain, and practice your rules, protocols, and routines.

Establishing the rules and consequences: By establishing rules and consequences, you are setting the tone for the class. The rules are necessary for survival, development, and learning. Once you have developed the rules, you must establish the consequences for breaking the rules. These consequences should be appropriate to your particular teaching situation and should not be interruptive to the instructional process.

Participate in the rule development activity (see Application 1).

Lesson Description: 4

Instructor's Responsibilities & Roles	Preservice Teacher's Responsibilities & Roles

Instructional Phase

In order to create and maintain a positive, structured learning environment in which ample practice opportunities are provided, you will need to develop and teach lesson protocols and routines to reduce or prevent injury, wasted time, and misbehavior. Remember, students must practice and learn each protocol you develop.

Participate in Application 2–protocol development.

Application(S)

1. Develop the rules and consequences. Explain why the rules are necessary. State rules positively. Avoid the "don'ts" and the "nots." Keep the number of rules to a minimum– (no more than seven). Post rules in an attractive and easily readable fashion. Develop a series of consequences (i.e., verbal warning, alone time, and developing a behavioral management plan).

1. Develop a rules/consequence poster following the guidelines. The poster should be attractive and easy to read.

2. Develop the lesson protocols:
   -Starting the lesson.
   -During the lesson.
   -Ending the lesson.

2. Develop a list of protocols: What the students are to do when they arrive. How to get the needed equipment and handle it. How you will get the students' attention to provide instruction. How you will quickly assign groups. How to put the equipment away. What to do at the end of the lesson for closure.

3. Create activities that allow students to practice the rules and lesson protocols.

3. Develop a set of activities to teach each rule and consequence and the associated protocols.

4. Implement those activities during one week.

4. Implement these activities during the next week.

5. Teach the same lesson plan.

5. Teach the same lesson.

6. Tape and analyze this teaching episode.

6. Tape and analyze the video, using observational software looking at teacher and student behaviors.

7. Compare the two analyses on teaching behaviors and student behaviors.

7. Compare the two analyses of teaching and student behaviors.

Lesson Description: 4

Instructor's Responsibilities & Roles

Preservice Teacher's Responsibilities & Roles

Lesson Closure

Review the findings of the analyses.

Establishing structure is essential to effective teaching and learning. Effective teachers become effective managers who establish, teach, and provide opportunities to practice the rules, protocols, and routines of the physical education classroom.

Participate in the discussion.

Lesson Reflection and Extensions

1. This lesson focused on the importance of management in the physical education classroom. Through analysis of teaching episodes, preservice teachers are able to realize the importance of establishing structure.
2. As a result of the implementation of this lesson plan, preservice teachers have indicated that practicing and teaching the rules and protocols of their class is very essential to maintaining the smooth pace of the lesson. "My students were so in tune to what was going on in my class. They were able to perform the activities with minimal disruptions because they knew their responsibilities."

Lesson Focus: 5
NASPE/NCATE Standard 5 – Communication

Topic	Developing a variety of ways to communicate information.
Cross-Reference	NASPE/NCATE Standard 5 - Outcome 5.2
Lesson Objectives	Preservice teachers will design an information bulletin board to post the rules and consequences and other information in the gymnasium. Preservice teachers will develop cue cards, including clip art and graphics, to help students understand how to perform the skill being presented. Preservice teachers will create a *PowerPoint* presentation to use when teaching a specific skill. This presentation will include the breakdown of the skill, including digital photographs and video clips that model how to perform the skill correctly.
Lesson Summary	Preservice teachers will design materials to communicate managerial and instructional information in a variety of ways. They will develop laminated posters of the rules and consequences that can be placed on a bulletin board. They also will develop a *PowerPoint* presentation and cue cards to use when teaching a specific skill.
PE Equipment Requirements	Plastic bat Basketball Batting tee Tennis racket Plastic ball Tennis ball Soccer ball Volleyball
Technology Requirements	Computers Microsoft *PowerPoint* software Digital cameras with video capabilities (if video is not available, just use the still frames) Camera software loaded onto the computers to download pictures 3 1/2 inch formatted disks Poster maker software Clip art Laminating machine
Other	Rule and consequence guideline poster Likert scale peer evaluation form (for presentation) *PowerPoint* how-to handout

Alignment of Standards: 5

NASPE/NCATE BTS

Standard 5
Communication
Outcome 5.2
Communicate managerial and instructional information in a variety of ways.

NETS–T

Standard II
Planning and Designing Learning Environments and Experiences
Outcome II-A
Design developmentally appropriate learning opportunities that apply technology-enhanced instructional strategies to support the diverse needs of learners.

Standard III
Teaching, Learning, and the Curriculum
Outcome III-B
Use technology to support learner-centered strategies that address the diverse needs of students.

Lesson Description: 5

Instructor's Responsibilities & Roles	Preservice Teacher's Responsibilities & Roles

Pre-Instructional Phase

Assign preservice teachers to bring in rules, protocols, etc., that have been posted on physical education websites and used by physical educators.	Locate and print out at least five sets of rules, protocols, etc., that have been posted on physical education websites and used by physical educators.
Make available all of the tools required for the lesson (see physical education requirements and technology requirements above).	

Instructional Phase

Teachers usually spend the first few weeks of school explaining, and having students practice, rules and routines in order to establish structure in the learning environment. During these first few weeks, effective teachers become effective managers who establish, teach, and provide opportunities to practice the rules, protocols, and routines of the physical education classroom. You were to bring in at least five different sets of rules, protocols, and consequences that have been posted on various physical education websites. Let's share some of your findings. Some of the rules have been established for secondary students and others have been established for elementary students. Now we are going to compare/contrast the sets of rules and consequences for each group.	Share the rules, protocols, and consequences found on different webpages and participate in the discussion.

Lesson Description: 5

Instructor's Responsibilities & Roles	Preservice Teacher's Responsibilities & Roles
Instructional Phase	
[Refers to Application activity 1.] When writing rules and consequences, remember the age group you are working with. Some rule writing guidelines that you can use are: 1. State rules positively. 2. Keep the number of rules to a minimum. 3. Post the rules in an attractive manner.	Participate in Application 1 (described in Application section).
One of the first skills you will acquire as a beginning teacher is to be able to provide the initial instruction of how to perform a skill. Providing effective instruction for your students is essential if learning is to occur. When giving instruction: 1. Limit it to one idea at a time. 2. Keep it brief. 3. Use cue words. 4. Include visuals (not all students are verbal learners).	Participate in Application 2 (described in Application section).
Application(S)	As preservice teachers proceed through these activities, they need to be active and ask questions when necessary.
Application activity 1: 1. Using the rules located during the homework assignment, preservice teachers are to develop a set of rules and consequences for an elementary level physical education class. Direct the preservice teachers to follow the guidelines. To model what you teach, develop a guideline poster and make it visible for all to see. 2. Make the poster attractive and easy to read. 3. Laminate the poster.	Application activity 1: 1. Following the guidelines, create a rules and consequences poster(s). 2. Add clip art, graphics, color, etc., to make it attractive. 3. Laminate the poster.

Lesson Description: 5

Instructor's Responsibilities & Roles	Preservice Teacher's Responsibilities & Roles

Application(S)

Application activity 2:
1. Place preservice teachers in groups of two.
2. Instruct preservice teachers on how to use *PowerPoint*, providing an information handout.
3. Assign preservice teachers to a specific skill [basketball dribble, two-hand strike (batting), volleyball underhand serve, tennis serve, soccer kick] and have them develop cues to use when teaching the skill to fifth graders.
4. Create text slides of the following using *PowerPoint*:
   -Overview of the skill.
   -Skill breakdown emphasizing the teachable cue (one slide for each cue used).
   -Question review.
5. Using the digital cameras, one partner is the demonstrator, the other is the camera operator. Take a still shot emphasizing each cue identified in the text slide.
6. Using the digital camera, video a short demonstration of how to perform the entire skill.
7. Following the instructions on the information handout, insert the still frames and the video clip into your presentation on the appropriate slides.
8. Personalize the presentation by adding color, backgrounds animation, etc.

Application activity 2:
1. Work in pairs.
2. Follow handout as to how to access *PowerPoint*.
3. Create cues for performing the skill assigned.
4. Create text slides.
5. Take still shots that emphasize the cues.
6. Video the skill.
7. Insert the pictures.
8. Following the directions in the handout, add personal touches to the presentation.

Lesson Description: 5

Instructor's Responsibilities & Roles	Preservice Teacher's Responsibilities & Roles

Lesson Closure

Each pair of students provides the introductory part of a skill lesson using their *PowerPoint* presentation.

Not all students learn in the same fashion. Some are visual learners, some are auditory learners, and some are kinesthetic learners. When you present information, you need to do so in an attractive manner, using various methods of presentation, and keeping it brief and to the point.

If you drag on and spend all of your time talking, then you will lose the students' attention. You must follow the KISS principle. What do you think that stands for? {Keep it short and simple!}

Evaluate their peers using the Likert scale evaluation form, rating the presentation on neatness, attractiveness, and appropriate content.

Participate in the discussion.

Lesson Reflection and Extensions

1. This lesson not only involves the preservice teachers in developing artifacts that can be used in teaching episodes, but also provides an opportunity for the preservice teachers to present their material in class.
2. The peer evaluation form provides a form of accountability for all students to be engaged in the closure part of the lesson.
3. After completing this assignment, one preservice teacher said, "This activity made you really think about how to perform the underhand serve. We had to lay out how to perform the skill, not only in our heads, but also on paper. Then we had to develop a picture to model the correct way to do it. It started out being hard, but it really helped me in learning how to do the skill correctly myself."

Lesson Focus: 6
NASPE/NCATE Standard 6 – Planning & Instruction

Topic	Lesson planning.
Cross-Reference	NASPE/NCATE Standard 6 - Outcome 6.4
Lesson Objectives	Preservice teachers will develop a comprehensive lesson plan outlining developmentally appropriate activities for second grade students based on the physical education program goals and objectives. Preservice teachers will integrate the use of technologies into the lesson plan. Preservice teachers will identify how to manage the use of these technologies in the lesson plan.
Lesson Summary	Preservice teachers will develop a comprehensive lesson plan for third grade students that focuses on a movement skill that is developmentally appropriate for this level. In this lesson plan, the preservice teachers will incorporate the use of CD/tape players, overhead projectors, and heart rate monitors.
PE Equipment Requirements	Music
Technology Requirements	Overhead projectors CD/tape players Heart rate monitors Computer with graphing and word processing software
Other	White sheets and/or projection screens

Alignment of Standards: 6

NASPE/NCATE BTS

Standard 6
Planning & Instruction
Outcome 6.1
Appropriate program and instructional goals.
Outcome 6.4
Designing learning experiences.

Standard 9
Technology
Outcome 9.2
Integrate technology.

NETS-T

Standard II
Planning and Designing Learning Environments and Experiences
Outcome II-A
Design developmentally appropriate learning opportunities that apply technology-enhanced instructional strategies to support the diverse needs of learners.
Outcome II-E
Plan strategies to manage student learning in a technology-enhanced environment.

Lesson Description: 6

Instructor's Responsibilities & Roles

Preservice Teacher's Responsibilities & Roles

Pre–Instructional Phase

Arrange to meet class in computer lab.

Make sure the computers have word processing and graphing capabilities.

Instructional Phase

Designing the learning experience through pre-instructional planning is an integral component of the teaching/learning process. Planning helps to ensure the implementation of an effective lesson, and ultimately an effective program.

Be attentive.

-Why plan? Any good physical education program begins with a good lesson plan. A strong lesson plan:

-Allows you to clarify.

-Allows you to stay focused.

-Provides a sense of organization and structure.

-Provides a permanent record of the lesson.

-Is your menu your guide to providing developmentally appropriate and individualized instruction?

Lesson Description: 6

	Instructor's Responsibilities & Roles	Preservice Teacher's Responsibilities & Roles
Instructional Phase	In developing daily lesson plans, you will not only focus on the content you plan to teach, but also on the organization and instructional decisions pertinent to effective teaching. The pre-instructional decisions made in the daily lesson plan include specific variations on individualizing your instruction, managing the environment, and outlining the intended competencies. Remember, the lesson plan is a detailed guide. Much thought and detail should go into it. The lesson plan should be written so that anyone could teach from it. Now we're going to design a lesson plan as a class. Your individual assignment will be to develop a lesson plan on your own. Choose the lesson plan format you will be using with your students and take them step-by-step through the process, writing their answers on the Board. Emphasize the importance of each section of your lesson plan and show the preservice teachers how to write objectives, instruction, and diagrams based on your own personal preferences.	Participate in the group discussion about completing a lesson plan as the instructor completes it on the board.

Lesson Description: 6

	Instructor's Responsibilities & Roles	**Preservice Teacher's Responsibilities & Roles**
Application(S)	Your lesson plan needs to be comprehensive follow the we did in class today. Make sure you include the following specific components in your lesson plan: -a comprehensive lesson plan for grade students focus on a movement skill (creative dance) that is developmentally appropriate for this level. -the use of CD/tape players, overhead projectors, and heart rate monitors. -many options using the equipment listed. The lesson should last 30 minutes and it should focus on rhythms and dance.	Complete a comprehensive lesson plan following the directions given by the instructor. The lesson plan focuses on a creative dance lesson in which the students use heart rate monitors to measure the intensity of their dance. The students create a dance using the overhead projector light to produce shadows on the wall. Preservice teachers can have the students teach each other their dances and/or evaluate each other. The preservice teachers make these decisions individually.
Lesson Closure	Pre-service teachers present highlights of their lesson plans, including the diagrams they used to emphasize class organization and show how they will manage the class when using the technology components of the lesson. Planning is a crucial part of the teaching process. Successful teachers plan effectively.	Present completed lesson plan.
Lesson Reflection and Extensions	1. This lesson focused on the preservice teachers developing lesson plans that incorporated technology for their students to use. 2. "When the professor showed us an example of the lesson plan that we were going to do, we freaked out. All of us were wondering, 'Why in the world would we have to plan like that just to teach physical education?' Now that I've done the planning, I'm thankful. I don't think I could have 'winged' it if I did not have such a detailed plan. Now that I've got a template, the lesson planning phase is so much easier."	

Lesson Focus: 7
NASPE/NCATE Standard 7 – Student Assessment

Topic	Self and peer assessment.
Cross-Reference	NASPE/NCATE Standard 7 - Outcome 7.3
Lesson Objectives	Preservice teachers will develop authentic self-evaluation sheets for fourth graders to use. Preservice teachers will create a spreadsheet for use on a personal digital assistant (PDA) for students to use in peer evaluation. Preservice teachers will develop a basketball lesson plan that incorporates the authentic self-evaluation sheets and the PDA peer assessments. Preservice teachers will implement the lesson plan.
Lesson Summary	Preservice teachers will develop a lesson plan that focuses on student assessment. In this lesson plan, they will teach the basketball dribble. After individual practice, partners will evaluate each other using the PDA program to record successful attempts based on the cues provided by the teacher. The preservice teachers also will develop a cognitive-based evaluation sheet for students to assess their knowledge of the skill. After the lesson plan has been approved, the preservice teachers will implement the lesson plan.
PE Equipment Requirements	Basketball Cones
Technology Requirements	Personal digital assistants Computer with word processing software PDA spreadsheet program Clip art
Other Requirements	None

Alignment of Standards: 7

NASPE/NCATE BTS

Standard 6
Planning and Instruction
Outcome 6.9
Develop and use appropriate instructional cues and prompts to facilitate competent motor skill performance.

Standard 7
Student Assessment
Outcome 7.3
Involve students in self and peer assessment.

NETS-T

Standard IV
Assessment and Evaluation
Outcome IV-A
Apply technology in assessing student learning of subject matter using a variety of assessment techniques.

Lesson Description: 7

	Instructor's Responsibilities & Roles	Preservice Teacher's Responsibilities & Roles
Pre-Instructional Phase	Assign students to develop the cues for the basketball dribble and bring them to class. Arrange for use of computers and PDAs. Establish a teaching environment for preservice teachers to implement the lesson plan (this could be a peer teaching environment or an environment with children).	Develop the cues for the basketball dribble.
Instructional Phase	An integral part of the teaching/learning process is assessment. You are responsible for assessing what students have learned in physical education, based on the goals and objectives you have set for your program. Assessment is a way to sample student performance to obtain information or to provide feedback about learning targets in order to make decisions and help improve the quality of learning. When you think of assessment what comes to mind? Assessment can be a formal process, such as written tests or skills tests, or it can be informal with you mercly observing and analyzing student performance.	Participate in discussion and answer questions.

Lesson Description: 7

Instructor's Responsibilities & Roles

Preservice Teacher's Responsibilities & Roles

Instructional Phase

Assessment has several different roles:
1. To enhance performance.
2. To provide information on class progress.
3. To evaluate instruction and the program.
4. To be an instructional tool.

Since the first step in the teaching process is to determine what your students should know and be able to do, you need to assess their performance to determine if they have met your objectives.

There are several different types of tests with which you are probably familiar:
1. Written tests.
2. Skills tests.
3. Fitness tests.

There also are performance-based assessments. Often these are called authentic assessments because to they occur in daily, real-life situations. There are many options providing authentic assessments in your daily classroom environment:
1. Teacher observation.
2. Peer observation.
3. Self-observation.
4. Student drawings.
5. Student journals.
6. Portfolios.

What do you think each type involves? Describe each type and provide an example.

Today we're going to focus on authentic types of assessments and create a lesson plan that utilizes what you create.

Lesson Description: 7

	Instructor's Responsibilities & Roles	Preservice Teacher's Responsibilities & Roles
Application(s)	1. Based on the cues you brought in for the basketball dribble, develop a self-assessment form that tests the students' cognitive knowledge about the skill. You can include graphics, drawings, and questions for them to answer. 2. Using the spreadsheet software, create a checklist that contains five opportunities. At the top of each column, identify the cue. Students are to place a check mark if they observed that cue for the opportunity and leave the column blank if they did not observe it. 3. Download the peer assessment checklist onto the PDA by placing the PDA into the cradle and performing a hotsync. 4. Develop a lesson plan that focuses on the basketball dribble. Include student use of the PDAs and the self-assessment checklist. Remember to provide practice opportunities before assessments take place. 5. Implement the lesson plan so students can actually use the assessments.	1. Using the word processor, create a self-assessment form for students to use. 2. Use the spreadsheet software to create the peer assessment checklist. 3. Download the peer assessment checklist onto the PDA. 4. Create a lesson plan following the instructor's template. Include the assessment pieces in the lesson plan. 5. Implement the lesson plan.
Lesson Closure	Review why assessment is so crucial to the teaching/learning process. Review the different types of assessments by having the preservice teachers answer deductive questions based on the purposes of the different types of assessments.	Participate in the discussion.
Lesson Reflection and Extensions	This lesson focused on the importance of student assessment in physical education. Since physical education is often seen as a marginalized curriculum, student assessment adds a measure of accountability. Through this activity, preservice teachers develop self and peer evaluation sheets and implement them in a teaching/learning environment.	

Lesson Focus: 8
NASPE/NCATE Standard 8 – Reflection

Topic	Teacher reflection.
Cross-Reference	NASPE/NCATE Standard 8 - Outcome 8.1
Lesson Objectives	Preservice teachers will become reflective practitioners, incorporating technology into the reflective cycle process. Preservice teachers will develop a reflective portfolio of their teaching performance.
Lesson Summary	Preservice teachers will develop an electronic portfolio that includes teaching artifacts and evidence of teaching improvements, including goals.
PE Equipment Requirements	None
Technology Requirements	Computers Video-capture software *PowerPoint* software
Other	Video of preservice teacher teaching Example of reflective portfolio Reflective Cycle Handout Reflective log template for *PowerPoint*

Alignment of Standards: 8

NASPE/NCATE BTS

Standard 8
Reflection
Outcome 8.1
Use a reflective cycle involving description of teaching, justification of the teaching performance, critique of the teaching performance, the setting of teaching goals, and implementation of changes.

NETS-T

Standard V
Productivity and Professional Practice
Outcome V-B
Continually evaluate and reflect on professional practice to make informed decisions regarding the use of technology in support of student learning.

Lesson Description: 8

Instructor's Responsibilities & Roles	Preservice Teacher's Responsibilities & Roles

Pre-Instructional Phase

Arrange to use computers with *PowerPoint* software. Develop handouts for class.	Videotape yourself teaching a class prior to this lesson.

Instructional Phase

Not only do effective teachers make decisions relating to planning, establishing structure, and providing feedback, they also reflect on the decisions they make and what happens in their classes as a result of those decisions. According to NASPE, reflective teachers evaluate the effects of the decisions they make and the effect of their actions on others. This reflection serves as a guide to future actions and decisions. Distribute handout of reflective cycle. The reflective process is an ongoing process in which decisions are based on the reflections about what has occurred in the classroom previously. The first step in becoming a reflective practitioner is to begin thinking about what you did, what your students did, the decisions you made in your classes, and why they all occurred.	Be attentive and participate in the discussion.

Lesson Description: 8

	Instructor's Responsibilities & Roles	**Preservice Teacher's Responsibilities & Roles**
Application(S)	1. Open a blank *PowerPoint* document. 2. Think about the lesson you taped and answer the following questions in bullet format on the slides (one question per slide). -Was the lesson plan followed? If not, why? -What happened in the class and why? -What were the strengths of the lesson and why? -What were the weaknesses of the lesson and why? -Was the material important to the students? If so, what made it important? -Did I interact with the students, providing feedback? -What do I need to do differently next time? -Was I successful in my teaching? Why? 3. Using the video capture software, watch your video and select clips that are representative of your answers. Insert those clips into the presentation on the appropriate slides. 4. On the last slide, set a goal(s) for improvement for the next time you teach. 5. Re-teach the lesson and videotape it. 6. Select a clip that provides evidence of the changes you made during the lesson from the first time to this time.	Complete the *PowerPoint* portfolio by following the directions of the instructor and the handout.
Lesson Closure	Review the reflective cycle.	Participate in the discussion.
Lesson Reflection and Extensions	This activity focused on the reflective process. Through this activity, preservice teachers developed a reflection portfolio that evaluated their teaching performances then retaught the lesson, making the necessary changes to make the lesson more successful.	

Lesson Focus: 9
NASPE/NCATE Standard 9 – Technology

Topic	Integrating technology into the physical education classroom.
Cross-Reference	NASPE/NCATE Standard 9 - Outcome 9.2
Lesson Objectives	Preservice teachers will design a lesson plan that incorporates the use of technologies into the lesson.
Lesson Summary	Preservice teachers will develop a lesson plan that incorporates the use of technologies into a dance lesson.
PE Equipment Requirements	Dance props (balls, hoops, streamers, scarves, rhythm sticks, etc.)
Technology Requirements	Computers Heart rate monitors Graphing software *Dance Dance Revolution* video games PlayStation platforms Televisions
Other	None

Alignment of Standards: 9

NASPE/NCATE BTS

Standard 6
Planning and Instruction
Outcome 6.6
Provide learning experiences that allow students to integrate knowledge and skills from multiple subject areas.

Standard 9
Technology
Outcome 9.2
Design, develop, and implement student learning activities that integrate information technology.

NETS-T

Standard II
Planning and Designing Learning Environments and Experiences
Outcome II-A
Design developmentally appropriate learning opportunities that apply technology-enhanced instructional strategies to support the diverse needs of learners.
Outcome II-D
Plan for the management of technology resources within the context of learning activities.
Outcome II-E
Plan strategies to manage student learning in a technology-enhanced environment.

Lesson Description: 9

Instructor's Responsibilities & Roles	Preservice Teacher's Responsibilities & Roles
Pre-Instructional Phase	
Provide sample lesson plans and a how to write measurable objectives handout. Give them to preservice teachers for review before this lesson.	Review the handout on how to write lesson plans and measurable objectives.
Develop the lesson plan template to be used.	
Develop the scenario for the lesson plans that are to be developed.	
Arrange for the class to have access to computers with graphing capabilities and word processing capabilities.	
Instructional Phase	
Why is planning such an integral part of the teaching process?	Participate in the discussion by answering questions.
Planning is important because it provides you with a detailed guide when implementing the lesson.	
What items should you have in your lesson plan?	
Measurable objectives.	
Organizational diagrams.	
Cues (refinements).	
Progression of activities.	
Introduction and review.	
Closure.	
Extensions.	
Applications.	

Lesson Description: 9

Instructor's Responsibilities & Roles

Preservice Teacher's Responsibilities & Roles

Instructional Phase

When planning a lesson, you need to take the time to write out the details and "leave no stone unturned" if possible. In the lesson plan, you are making decisions regarding managerial issues, teaching strategies, checking for understanding, content, assessment tools, and feedback that should be given. The lesson plan should be written so that anyone could teach from it. It represents a detailed record of what you intend to do and have your students do in your class.

Since we are in the age of technology and both we and our students must meet national technology standards, we will begin to incorporate student use of technology into our lesson plans. When you think of technology what naturally comes to mind? Of course, computers. But technology encompasses so much more. It includes televisions, VCRs, CD players, DVDs, tape players, cameras, heart rate monitors, pedometers, and more. The list goes on and on. Let's create a comprehensive list of technologies we can use in physical education.

Participate by adding examples of technology that can be incorporated into physical education.

Lesson Description: 9

Instructor's Responsibilities & Roles	Preservice Teacher's Responsibilities & Roles
Application(S)	
1. You and your colleague are the physical educators at Creekside Elementary. So far your fifth grade dance unit has been successful, but you want to add some flair to boost the students' interest in dancing. In recent conversations with children and your observations at the local mall, you deduct that the new video craze is a full-body video game that incorporates dance, *Dance Dance Revolution*, otherwise known to the students as DDR. You and your colleague decide that this is a major possibility for your dance unit. Both of you purchase the game. Thanks to the generosity of some of your parents, you were able to use six television sets, six PlayStation platforms, and six DDR games. The class has 24 students, so this works out nicely for stations.	1. Listen and take notes about the scenario.
2. You are charged with developing the lesson plan for the dance unit. You also have 24 heart rate monitors and access to the dance steps of the DDR dances (www.ddrfreaks.com).	2. Develop the lesson plan following the specifics provided.
3. In addition to developing the lesson plan, you will need to develop a graph based on the data collected from the heart rate monitors. The DDR game also collects data from the performances. Create a graph using those data as an example for the students.	3. Develop a sample graph of the data that will be collected to show the students.

Lesson Description: 9

Instructor's Responsibilities & Roles

Preservice Teacher's Responsibilities & Roles

Lesson Closure	Review the importance of lesson planning. Review the many different types of technologies that can be used in the physical education classroom.	Participate in the discussion.
Lesson Reflection and Extensions	This lesson focused on the preservice teacher developing a lesson plan that incorporated student use of technology in the classroom. Most people think that technology only involves the use of computers. This lesson plan looked at how a child's video game could be used in the physical education environment.	

Lesson Focus: 10
NASPE/NCATE Standard 10 – Collaboration

Topic	Advocacy website development.
Cross-Reference	NASPE/NCATE Standard 10 - Outcome 10.1
Lesson Objectives	Preservice teachers will develop a website that advocates a pretend physical education program.
Lesson Summary	Preservice teachers will develop a website that provides information about and advocates for a physical education program.
PE Equipment Requirements	None
Technology Requirements	Computers Website development software Clip art, graphics, photographs Internet access
Other	None

Alignment of Standards: 10

NASPE/NCATE BTS

Standard 9
Technology
Outcome 9.1
Demonstrate knowledge of current technology and its applications to physical education.
Standard 10
Collaboration
Outcome 10.1
Identify strategies to become an advocate in the school and community to promote a variety of physical activity opportunities.

NETS-T

Standard V
Productivity and Professional Practice
Outcome V-D
Use technology to communicate and collaborate with peers, parents, and the larger community in order to nurture student learning.

Lesson Description: 10

Instructor's Responsibilities & Roles	Preservice Teacher's Responsibilities & Roles
Pre-Instructional Phase Arrange for access to computers with webpage development software. Develop a checklist of materials needed to place on the web page. These items may include: clip art, links to physical education websites, links to health association websites, data that support the need for instruction in physical education and participation in physical activity, recreation department links and/or addresses, descriptions of your pretend program (including mission statement and goals/objectives), links to local events that support awareness for physical activity needs, and links to national physical education standards. Develop a rubric for preservice teachers to use to evaluate their website.	Locate the materials on the checklist. Identify the websites and places you can find the information needed to place on your website. Develop a mission statement and some broad goals for your program.
Instructional Phase Teaching is a professional responsibility in which you foster relationships with others, especially your students. Establishing positive relationships is vital to the future of the physical education profession. If you want your students, parents, administrators, and others to understand and support your program, you must establish positive relationships that emphasize the importance of physical education to the development of the whole child and to the total school curriculum.	Participate in the discussion.

Lesson Description: 10

	Instructor's Responsibilities & Roles	Preservice Teacher's Responsibilities & Roles
Instructional Phase	Unfortunately, many people still do not associate physical education with student health and future participation in physical activities. Share your philosophy and your program, emphasizing that the ultimate goal is to help students become physically educated individuals and to prepare them for a lifetime of involvement in physical activity. One way to share your information is to provide it via the Internet. More and more people have access to the Internet. By providing information about your program and showing others how your program can contribute to the national health goals laid out in Healthy People 2010, you are establishing a positive relationship with parents, students, administrators, politicians, etc.	
Application(S)	1. Develop a website including the materials listed in the pre-instructional phase. 2. Follow these guidelines and create others to establish positive relationships when developing your website: -Explain the importance of physical education. -Share your philosophy and program. -Advertise special events occurring in your program (e.g., PTA performances, Jump Rope for Heart). -Express appreciation to all who have helped. 3. Customize your website by adding clip art, pictures, graphics, word art, background colors, etc. 4. Evaluate your website using the rubric.	Complete the assignment, following the directions.

Lesson Description: 10

	Instructor's Responsibilities & Roles	Preservice Teacher's Responsibilities & Roles
Lesson Closure	Preservice teachers present their websites in a poster presentation format. Half of the class show their websites while the other half view the websites and take notes about the special features and qualities of each site. Then the groups switch roles.	Examine the different websites and take notes about the special features and qualities of each site.

Present your own website and answer questions about it. |
| **Lesson Reflection and Extensions** | The preservice teachers developed a website advocating their own mock physical education programs. Through this activity, preservice teachers gained experience in using web page development software and attractively presenting material on the importance of physical education. | |

Note: NETS-T reprinted with permission from the National Education Technology Standards, ©2002, ISTE (International Society for Technology in Education), 800.336.5191 (U.S. & Canada) or 541.302.3777 (Int'l), iste@iste.org, www.iste.org. All rights reserved. Permission does not constitute an endorsement by ISTE. For more information about the NETS Project, contact Lajeane Thomas, Director, NETS Project, 318.257.3923, lthomas@latech.edu.

References

International Society for Technology in Education. (2000). *National education technology standards for teachers.* Eugene, OR: ISTE.

National Association for Sport and Physical Education. (2001). *Standards for initial programs in physical education teacher education.* Reston, VA: Author. Available at: http://www.aahperd.org/naspe/pdf_files/standards_initial.pdf.

Soar, R. and Soar, R. (1979). Emotional climate and management. In P. Peterson and H. Walberg (Eds.), *Research on teaching: Concepts, findings and implications.* Berkley, CA: McCutchan Publishing.

Web Resources

Association Websites

American Alliance for Health, Physical Education, Recreation, and Dance
http://www.aahperd.org/

American Cancer Society
http://www.cancer.org/

American Council on Exercise
http://www.acefitness.org/

American Diabetes Association
http://www.diabetes.org/main/application/commercewf

American Dietetic Association
http://www.eatright.org/

American Heart Association
http://www.americanheart.org/

British Heart Foundation
http://www.bhf.org.uk/youngpeople/index.asp?secondlevel=397&thirdlevel=407

Centers for Disease Control
http://www.cdc.gov/

Cooper Institute
http://www.cooperinst.org/ftgmain.asp

International Society for Technology in Education
http://www.iste.org

Physical Best – American Fitness Alliance
http://www.americanfitness.net/Physical_Best/

President's Council on Physical Fitness & Sports
http://www.fitness.gov/

Educational Websites

Can Teach PE Lesson Resources
http://www.canteach.ca/links/linkpelesson.html

Educational Teacher Software Download Center
http://www.teach-nology.com/downloads/

Free Things for Educators
http://www.freethings4educators.com/

Healthy Schools.net
http://www.healthyschools.net/

Hoops for Heart
http://www.americanheart.org/presenter.jhtml?identifier=2441

Jump Rope for Heart
http://www.americanheart.org/presenter.jhtml?identifier=2360

MegaEd: Physical Education
http://www.megaed.com/pe.htm

North Carolina Physical Education is… ACTIVE
http://www.beactivenc.org/8.html

Nutrition Navigator
http://navigator.tufts.edu/index.html

PE Central
http://pe.central.vt.edu/

PE Lesson Plan Page
http://members.tripod.com/~pazz/lesson.html

PE Links 4U
http://www.pelinks4u.org

PE Zone
http://reach.ucf.edu/~pezone/

Physical Education Digest
http://www.pedigest.com/

Physical Education Lesson Plans
http://schools.eastnet.ecu.edu/pitt/ayden/
PHYSED8.HTM

Special Olympics
http://www.specialolympics.org/

Sport Media
http://www.sports-media.org/

Tech Newsletter
http://pesoftware.com/news.html

The Heart
http://sln.fi.edu/biosci/heart.html

Product Website Resource

Academic Superstore
http://www.academicsuperstore.com

Bonnie's Fitware Inc
http://www.pesoftware.com

Brockport Physical Fitness Test
http://www.humankinetics.com/products/
search.cfm

CNET Software Downloads
http://www.cnet.com

Cramer Sports Medicine Catalog
http://www.cramersportsmed.com/
institutional_catalog.jsp?catID=114

HyperStudio
http://www.hyperstudio.com/

Microscribe Publishing
http://www.microscribepub.com

Mobile Database
http://www.mobiledb.com/

Polar Heart Rate Monitors
http://www.polar.fi/

Road Runner Sports
http://www.roadrunnersports.com

Tournament Builder and Other Sports Software
http://www.polevault.com/trackandfieldstore/
main.html

Tucows Software Downloads
http://www.tucows.com

ZDNet Software Downloads
http://www.zdnet.com

Websites for PK–12 Students

EduHound
http://www.eduhound.com/

Families on the Move
http://www.niagarahearthealth.com/families/
table_of_content.htm

Health Finder for Kids
http://www.healthfinder.gov/kids/

Kids 'N Fitness
http://exchange.co-nect.net/Teleprojects/project/
Fitness

Kids and Teens Health
http://dmoz.org/Kids_and_Teens/Health/Fitness/

Kids Health
http://kidshealth.org/index.html

SmartPlay
http://www.smartplay.net/

Tone Teen
http://www.toneteen.com/

Index

Physical Education and Training–
    Computer-Assisted Instruction

A guide for integrating technology into instructional experiences for the physical education teacher education curriculum.

This book shows the alignment between NASPE Beginning Teacher Standards and NETS-T technology standards. These standards are directed to minimum acceptable teaching competencies for beginning teachers.

The book provides lesson plans for integrating technology and physical education curriculum. Also, the lesson plan examples can be modified to meet any number of lesson objectives.

Melanie Mitchell, Ph.D.

Department of Health, Leisure, and Exercise Science
Appalachian State University

Robert N. McKethan, Ed.D.

Department of Health, Leisure, and Exercise Science
Appalachian State University

ISBN 1-893166-99-6
52495

9 781893 166998

DATE DUE